Clearing away the Rubbish

ADRIAN PLASS

with illustrations by W James Hammond

MINSTREL
Eastbourne

First published 1988
Reprinted 1988
Reprinted 1989

*Front cover and page design by W James Hammond
Music manuscript by Gerry Page*

The music for the following songs is
reproduced by kind permission of the copyright holders:
I Didn't Have to See You and *There Won't Be Time
Tonight* music by Paul Winter; *Hallelujah in the
Back of My Mind* by James Hammond.

British Library Cataloguing in Publication Data

Plass, Adrian
Clearing away the rubbish.
I. Title
821'.914

ISBN 1-85424-025-0 (Minstrel)
0-7324-0400-2 (Albatross)

Printed in Great Britain for
Minstrel, an imprint of Monarch Publications Ltd,
Lottbridge Drove, Eastbourne, E Sussex BN23 6NT by
Richard Clay Ltd, Bungay, Suffolk.
Typeset by CST, Eastbourne.

Contents

Performing Licence   9
Preface   11

REALITY IS ROTTEN!
1.   Christian Confession   15
2.   Our Times   21
3.   Bee   25
4.   The Apathetic Creed   29
5.   The Weather   31

PASSION PROHIBITED!
1.   The Preacher   41
2.   Salt of the Earth   45

PROMOTE PARTY SPIRIT!
1.   Hallelujah in the Back of My Mind   51
2.   Anagrams   55
3.   The Well   59

MISERY IS MANIFOLD!
1.   Growbag World   67
2.   Poison Pools   69
3.   Shell   71
4.   When Does the Joy Start?   73

PERFECTION IS POSSIBLE!
1.   The Law   79
2.   I Found a Bird   83
3.   I Didn't Have to See You   87

CALLOUS CREATOR!
1.   My Baby   93
2.   Why Did He Choose?   97
3.   Letter to God—and God's Reply   101

FEELING IS FAILING!

1. Hall of Mirrors
   When I Was a Small Boy 107
2. Nice 111
3. Stress 117
4. There Won't Be Time Tonight 121

MARVELLOUS ME!

1. Phone Call 127
2. Shoes 131
3. Operation 137

CONFORMING IS CORRECT!

1. The Real Problem 141
2. Legs 145
3. God Says 149

WORLDLINESS IS WONDERFUL!

1. My Way 157
2. Machine 161
3. Party
   Dream of Being Special 163

CUT-PRICE CHRISTIANITY!

1. When I Became a Christian 173
2. Books 179
3. Nathan Rap 183
4. Away in a Gutter
   A Father Knows No Sadness 187
5. Snowdon 191

HOPE IS HOPELESS!

1. Hope Poems: Daffodils; Gatwick Airport;
   Winter Walk; I Watch 201
2. Shades of Blue 207
3. I Want to Be with You 209
4. Letter to Lucifer 215

I am indebted to my wife, Bridget, for preserving what sanity I have by organising and editing the material in this book with such talent and efficiency.

Performing Licence

If you wish to perform any of the pieces in this book, you are free to do so without charge, provided the performance is undertaken in an amateur context. The purchase of this book constitutes a licence granting the right to perform the pieces for no financial gain.

This licence does not grant you permission to reproduce the text in any way; such permission must be sought from the publisher (see copyright notice at the front of the book).

The piece *My Way* (based on a song by Paul Anka and used by permission of Intersong Music Ltd) may be performed only by members of the Performing Rights Society.

Those wishing to engage in professional or commercial performances should make a separate approach to the author's agent, Mr Darley Anderson, 11 Eustace Road, London NW6.

All film, video and audio recording and broadcasting rights are reserved by the publisher.

You will be happy! You will be happy! You will be happy! Sing up!

Preface

I BECAME A Christian when I was sixteen years old, but it wasn't until I was thirty-seven that I absorbed an essential truth.

God is nice and he likes me.

This seemingly insubstantial fact revolutionised my life. I had juggled with spiritual superlatives and personal guilt for more than twenty years, without experiencing any lasting peace. It wasn't until I underwent emotional disintegration three years ago that God was able to reassemble me in a form that was able to perceive and accept the warm gentleness of his care for me.

Why did it take so long? What prevented me, and prevents many others, from finding out about God's love and sense of humour? Who stops us from relaxing in the confidence that we will never be rejected by him?

Over the last three years I have been learning some of the answers to these questions, and trying, through writing and speaking and performing, to pass them on to people who feel weighed down with guilt, and permanently twitchy with sin. Satan is constantly at work piling pieces of convincing-looking rubbish over the truth—anything to prevent us looking at Jesus.

We are all ratbags. None of us is able to reach the level of virtue that would earn us a place in heaven. That's why Jesus died.

This book is a collection of sketches, verse stories, songs, comments and ideas that attempt to expose and remove some of the rubbish that has accumulated over our faith. Please use them in your own situation. They are not exactly literary masterpieces, but if they make people feel a little more free, they'll have done their job.

**REALITY
IS ROTTEN!**

Christian Confession

TALKING ABOUT FAITH in its simplest form has always been a problem to me. I seem to double de-clutch into some strange religious gear that doesn't produce any forward movement at all. I think it has something to do with vocabulary and language habits. A friend of mine, after guest-preaching at a local church, was asked, 'May we fellowship in the petrol?' How did one whole section of the church end up communicating in this strange way? We're all just as bad, whichever denomination we attach ourselves to. We have our own little ways of speaking about and expressing our beliefs and spiritual ideas. That's why I find people like Gerald Coates, Gavin Reid and Jim Smith so refreshing. They sound like human beings when they talk about God. Different personalities they may be, but they are themselves, not good or bad copies of somebody else.

Often this difficulty with language, especially when coupled with a lack of passion, results in a statement of faith that sounds more like a confession of some awful sin than an announcement of salvation and eternal joy. I know. I've done it. I'm working towards being able to ignore the lie that says you can't express your faith in a natural and confident way.

Christian Confession requires just two people and a clipboard. The interviewer, armed with his questions, is a typical 'in depth' television reporter. His questions are couched in hushed, empathetic tones as he draws the awful truth from his nervous interviewee. George, twitching and embarrassed, reveals his dependency on Christianity as though he were confessing to drug addiction or sexual perversion. This sketch can be useful for launching discussions, and it really isn't too difficult to do. One of my own particular favourites.

Christian Confession

INTERVIEWER: George, you are a Christian?

GEORGE: Yeah, that is true. I am a convicted practisin' Christian.

INTERVIEWER: And how long have you been err . . . doing it?

GEORGE: Well, I've been one for a few years now, but I think I was actually one for a little while before that without really realisin' it.

INTERVIEWER: I see. So you weren't always—like you are now?

GEORGE: No, I was a normal kid, grew up like anybody else. Took drugs, got in trouble with the police, pinched stuff from me family and friends, beat a few people up at weekends, owed money all over the place, couldn't handle relationships, scared of the bomb, frightened of cancer, out of work, suicidal, couldn't sleep at night, couldn't stay awake durin' the day, confused about life, terrified of death, I was just your average bloke, I had everythin' goin' for me and I threw it all away.

INTERVIEWER: What happened?

GEORGE: Yeah, well . . . there was this party: If I'd known it was a Christian party—I mean, I'd never have gone. I'd always kept away from people like that in the past— Christians I mean. Course, I'd experimented with it. All kids do, don't they? The odd prayer behind the cricket pavilion, a bit of harmless worship with a couple of mates on the way home from school—I mean, it doesn't hurt anyone, does it?

INTERVIEWER: But the party was different?

GEORGE: Yeah . . . it was—different.

INTERVIEWER: In what way?

GEORGE: Well, I didn't notice anythin' at first. I was just happily gettin' drunk and makin' a nuisance of myself, like you do at parties, but after a while I suddenly realised that most of the people round me were . . . well, I might as well be frank about it—they were sober!

INTERVIEWER: How did that make you feel?

GEORGE: Well, I panicked at first. I mean, it was—it was really *blatant*, know what I mean? And some of them . . . they were . . .

INTERVIEWER: Yes?

GEORGE: They were smilin' at each other.

INTERVIEWER: They were smiling?

GEORGE: Yeah. I really wanted to get out, but someone pushed a tonic water in my hand and I just didn't seem to have any willpower. And then . . . then . . .

INTERVIEWER: Then?

GEORGE: This bloke—must've been a dealer I suppose. He had a load of tracts, and he gave me one, and I—I . . .

INTERVIEWER: And . . .?

GEORGE: I read it.

INTERVIEWER: You—read—a—tract?

GEORGE: Yeah!

INTERVIEWER: And then?

GEORGE: Well, someone pulled the blinds down and we started passin' a new testament around, and—I dunno—I just couldn't stop. I had to have more and more. I was crazy for it! I met this bloke at midnight behind the dairy the next night, just to pick up a couple of pages of Ezekiel. I was in a terrible state. And then, a few days later, it happened.

INTERVIEWER: What happened?

GEORGE: I—I lost the shakes. My hands stopped shaking. I couldn't make them shake any more, however hard I tried. I started to feel—clean and sort of healthy. I couldn't not sleep at night. I wasn't havin' nightmares. I can't describe it, it was . . . awful. But none of that was as bad as when I started . . .

INTERVIEWER: Go on . . .

GEORGE: I started bein' . . . good!

INTERVIEWER: What form did that take?

GEORGE: Well, it started with little things, you know. I found myself helpin' with the washin' up, passin' things to people without bein' asked—that sort of thing, but then it got worse and worse. I had this awful feelin' that I wasn't the most important person in the world, and people like [redacted] had as much right to live as I did . . .

INTERVIEWER: That's incredible!

GEORGE: I know, I know, but there was nothin' I could do about it! I was on the slippery slope to happiness, and I just didn't know how to stop!

INTERVIEWER: George, what made you do it? What attracted you to Christianity in the first place?

GEORGE: I know what it was! It was the superficial things, the tinselly, glitterin' things that somehow seemed so important.

INTERVIEWER: Such as?

GEORGE: Oh, you know—eternal life, total forgiveness, deep and permanent joy, a chance to find my place in the universe. I was fooled into thinkin' those things were the really important things. The *really* important things, like sex, and money, and power—I dunno, I just lost sight of 'em. You lose your perspective, you see.

INTERVIEWER: And now? Is there hope for you?

GEORGE: Well, I've been away to a—place, and had the err . . . the cure, and, well, I do feel a bit more hopeful now.

INTERVIEWER: There are some encouraging signs then?

GEORGE: Yes, I'm pleased to say that I *have* been swearin' at

my mother—I swore at her a little this mornin' actually—
apologised to her afterwards, I'm afraid, but they did say
at the—place, that it was bound to take time. I'm hoping
to form a little group over the next few days to beat up
people on their way home from church, so . . . you know,
slowly but surely . . .

INTERVIEWER: George—thank you.

GEORGE: Thank *you*.

Our Times

It TAKES A lot of courage to describe anything in this book as 'poetry'. On the shelf in front of me as I write are poetry collections by Stewart Henderson and Steve Turner. They are a constant inspiration to me—to write prose. Seriously though, a poem like Stewart's 'A Prophet and a Wet Thursday' is quite enough to remind me of my limitations in this area. In case anyone thinks this is false modesty I'd better add that I'm amazingly good at thousands of other things. I'm one of the slickest light bulb changers in our family, for instance.

I include *Our Times* for two reasons. First, it provides the reader with an interesting puzzle, and secondly, it illustrates the perils of straying into a field where people are throwing rubbish around in a rather subtle way.

Once, a long time ago, I joined a poetry circle. It met once every month so that members could read their new poems and receive criticism from the rest of the group. I only went twice.

On the first occasion I chickened out of taking any of my poems along. Like many other closet poets I believed, on the one hand, that my 'works' were probably a load of garbage, but at the same time I nursed a secret fierce hope that they were the product of genius. I didn't feel ready to expose that vulnerable little hope to the possibility of extinction yet, so I decided that for my first visit I would just sit and listen; assess the state of the market, as it were. The poems I heard had two things in common. They were almost totally incomprehensible, and they were just about impossible to respond to. As each one reached its sonorous end, people would either nod mournfully and say 'Mmmm . . .' or someone would declare with judicially restrained enthusiasm, 'I think I'd like to hear that again.'

Back at home I studied my own poetry sadly. It was totally flawed by comprehensibility. You could see what it meant at a glance. My only hope was that the members of the poetry circle didn't understand each other's poetry either. But how to test that theory? In the end I decided to take along the piece that I call *Our Times*, read it to the group, and see how they responded. At the next meeting I did exactly that. They were quite impressed, and I never went again.

See if you can guess where *Our Times* comes from. Clues? Well, it isn't a poem, and there's a strong hint in the title.

Our Times

Like the merchandise of Wells
The wise men state,
Chemical can put up the speed,
In part grassland, in all the fold.
Swirling ooze contains exotic bed of beastly fossil.
Literary corporal garlanded in Ireland,
Luck begins to change for a literary lady.
There's a sign chlorine is included
In nature terminology.
At once correct the tiny slant
Wine drunk to noisy Elsinore accompaniment,
Beetles learning to ride horses,
A plain sort of oyster.

Did you guess right? This 'poem' is the last ten consecutive clues from a *Times* crossword!

Bee

By way of contrast, I wrote this little rhyme when I was a small boy. I know it's a bit silly, but it embodies an acceptance and simplicity that are difficult to recapture as adulthood clamps in. Part of being born again must be the release of that childlike spirit. Perhaps, after a few more years, the Holy Spirit will make me real enough to write something like *Bee* again!

Bee

The world is very big and round
And in it many things are found
E.g.
A bee.

The Apathetic Creed

EVERY SUNDAY IN church I say the creed that begins: 'I believe in God the Father . . . .' Over the years I've learned to understand quite a lot of this awesome statement. I even genuinely mean quite a lot of it. I like to think that when I finally come face to face with Jesus the whole thing will flow through me, an explosive rush of ultimate knowledge about the Creator and his creation. In the meantime, an absolutely genuine expression of my creed would be a strange, Gruyere-cheese-like version of the original.

I suppose that's true for all of us; believers of different kinds, agnostics, atheists, we've all got a personal, idiosyncratic creed, that would look rather strange if it was publicly and honestly revealed.

The Apathetic Creed is a light-hearted list/exaggeration of the kinds of unthinking comment often heard from casual opponents of the Christian faith. Hopefully, it encourages Christians to take an honest look at their own *private* creeds. There's nothing wrong with doing that, any more than there's anything wrong with having a look round to see where you've got to in the middle of a journey.

It can be performed by one person, but is possibly more effective when delivered chorally and solemnly by a group. Why not try writing the creeds you might hear from other types of people?

The Apathetic Creed

I believe there is something out there, but I don't know if
   I'd call it God, more a sort of force.
Anyway you don't have to go to church to be a Christian.
What I say is, 'Who made God, anyway?'
What about all the suffering?
What about volcanoes?
And earthquakes.
And floods.
And famines.
And road accidents.
And Bob Monkhouse.
And depression.
And the bomb.
And cancer.
And AIDS.
And I believe the Bible contradicts itself—I don't know
   exactly where, but it does. It's common knowledge.
I rather like what the Buddhists say, or is it the Muslims,
   about getting into a state of real sort of peacefulness.
And I believe it's more important to be a good person than
   to believe in any specific religion, and most people who
   do are fanatics, and we all know what fanatics are like.
And I believe people shouldn't be indoctrinated into
   believing things, even if they're true.
And I believe that church is very, very boring . . .

The Weather

The Weather IS a bit of fun. But it's also a warning not to allow the games we've developed in our churches to obscure the reality that God's love is available in a very simple, uncluttered way.

Unlike some of the pieces in this book, it really does need careful rehearsal, especially the sections where 'responses' are involved.

NB Weather men change! Don't be afraid to change the sketch accordingly.

The Weather

A group of about ten people are seated on chairs, chatting animatedly as they wait for the meeting to begin. One person is looking self-conscious and unsure. He is here for the first time. After about ten seconds Brother Mervyn, the group leader, enters and takes up a standing position in front of the group. They stop chatting and sit attentively, waiting for him to begin the meeting.

BROTHER MERVYN: Well, good evening, Brothers and Sisters, and welcome to tonight's meeting of the Fifth Day Michael Fishites. *(Holds hand up above his head)* All hail and sleet to Michael Fish!

ALL: *(Fingertips meeting above heads)* May he, with Ian McGaskill and Bill Giles, forecast eternally.

BROTHER MERVYN: May the weather be with you.

ALL: As it was on Wednesday *(lower left hand)* is today *(lower right hand)* and will be on Friday, rain without end, a-gain *(all point forward on second syllable of 'a-gain')*

BROTHER MERVYN: We begin this morning by extending a warm but slightly breezy welcome to our new member, Gregory. *(Gestures towards Gregory)* Doubtless in a bit of a fog at the moment, but you'll soon become acclimatised, Brother Gregory.

(They all titter dutifully)

SISTER FELICITY: *(Sitting next to Gregory—speaks to him)* Brother Mervyn always says that when we have a new member, Brother Gregory.

BROTHER GREGORY: Oh, does he?

BROTHER MERVYN: Now, over to Sister Meryl for the notices. *(Sits)*

SISTER MERYL: *(Standing and referring to notes)* The 'sitting on the beach in pouring rain without umbrellas or coats club' will not be meeting next Tuesday as the forecast is for sunshine.

ALL: What a shame! Pity! Nuisance! Oh, dear! *etc.*

SISTER MERYL: As many of you know, Brother Bernard was out on Salisbury Plain last night. He was aiming to prove that, whatever the unmeteorological scoffers may say, it *is* possible to stand in the open in a bucket of water holding twenty pounds of explosives, be struck by lightning, and not only be unharmed, but actually be uplifted by the experience. We salute him for this great contribution to our cause.

(All applaud enthusiastically)

SISTER FELICITY: What happened?

SISTER MERYL: He's dead.

BROTHER CYRIL: We'll collect some money for him!

SISTER MERYL: We've got to collect *him* first. Finally, the collection for last week amounted to seventy-three pence. This will be donated to Brother Stanley, who sustained major damage after excessive wind on Tuesday night.

(She sits)

BROTHER MERVYN: Thank you, Sister, and now let us stand and lean for Twinkle, twinkle. Brother Earnest, if you please.

(All stand and lean over to one side. Brother Earnest beats rhythmically on the glass of a barometer held in some 'symbolic' fashion. All lean at the end of each line)

ALL: *(Singing)* Twinkle, twinkle little star, *(lean)*
                We don't wonder what you are, *(lean)*
                You're the cooling down of gases, *(lean)*
                Forming into solid masses. *(lean)*
                Twinkle, twinkle little star, *(lean)*

We don't wonder what you are.
   *(All trace a large circle with forefingers, arm extended fully
   upwards)*
ALL: *(Slowly and significantly as circles are traced)* I—so—bars!
   (All sit)
BROTHER MERVYN: And now, our reading from the Outlook
   according to Fish. *(Raises hand)* May the clouds part!
ALL: *(Stand)* Cumulo Nimbus!
BROTHER MERVYN: Alto Cirrus!
ALL: *(Sit)* Alto Nimbus!
BROTHER MERVYN: Cumulo Cirrus!
ALL: *(Standing)* Thick Fog!
   *(All sit. Brother Ambrose comes out to read from large book
   on lectern)*
BROTHER AMBROSE: *(In quavering, prophetic tones)* And Michael
   Fish did prophesy, saying, 'Behold, the heavens shall
   open and a deluge shall descend,' and it came to pass that
   no rain fell for many weeks, and they who did till the land
   did wax wrath against Michael Fish and did revile him,
   and Michael Fish did speak, saying, 'I can't get it right all
   the time,' and they did snort and leave him for a season,
   but those who truly believed wore wellies right through
   the drought. May Michael Fish be revered.
ALL: With Bill Giles let him be honoured.
BROTHER MERVYN: Yes, indeed. Wonderful words! And now,
   friends, I'd like us all to greet our new brother, Gregory,
   here today for the first time.
BROTHER GREGORY: Yes, I saw your postcard in the butchers.
ALL: *(With pleased significance)* Ah, the postcard! The postcard.
   Yes, the postcard!
BROTHER MERVYN: Brother Cyril, perhaps you'd introduce
   Brother Gregory to everyone.

BROTHER CYRIL: Yes, of course. Well, I'm Brother Cyril.

BROTHER GREGORY: Hello.

BROTHER CYRIL: And this is Brother Earnest Hummer.

BROTHER GREGORY: Okay, Earnest?

BROTHER EARNEST: *(Hums earnestly)* Mmmmmmm—mmmmmmmm . . .

BROTHER CYRIL: This is Sister Felicity. She can make a barometer stand up on its hind legs and beg!

BROTHER GREGORY: Really! I'd like to—to see that.

BROTHER CYRIL: You've seen Brother Ambrose, and this is Sister Laetitia. She runs our children's group.

SISTER LAETITIA: We call them 'The Little Drips'.

BROTHER GREGORY: Oh, how nice.

BROTHER MERVYN: Well now, Brother Gregory. Tell us about yourself. You obviously believe deeply in the weather. Is there a particular area that fascinates you?

BROTHER GREGORY: *(Shyly)* Well, I am very blessed by ground temperatures.

BROTHER MERVYN: *(Deeply moved)* Brother Gregory, I believe you have been sent to us for a very special reason. *(Continues in awestruck tones)* Sister Felicity has a special ministry in ground temperatures!
    (All react with amazement)

BROTHER CYRIL: *(He gets a bit excitable sometimes—jumps to his feet and waves his fist in the air)* All hail to the great Michael Fish, for he has done great things! Let the rain fall! Let the lightning flash! Let the thunder roar! Let the wind—

SISTER LAETITIA: Steady, Brother Cyril, that'll do. *(To Brother Gregory)* Brother Cyril is a bit fundamental. But he's so excited about this wonderful link between you and Sister Felicity. Soul mates in the exciting world of ground temperatures!

BROTHER GREGORY: *(Uneasily)* When I say *very* blessed, I don't mean—

SISTER FELICITY: *(With passion)* Brother Gregory, are there any little—problems you'd like to talk about? *(She leans towards him)*

BROTHER GREGORY: Well, I know you're keen on all kinds of weather, and—

SISTER FELICITY: *(She leans even closer)* Yes, indeed!

BROTHER GREGORY: Well, I've often wanted to join a group like this, but . . . I hardly know how to say this . . .

SISTER FELICITY: *(She leans horribly close)* Yes?

BROTHER GREGORY: *(Shame-faced)* Well—I'm afraid I lack humidity.

ALL: Ah! Yes! Mmmmm . . . *etc. (Sister Felicity 'comforts' him)*

BROTHER MERVYN: Brother Gregory, believe me when I say that many of us in this room have suffered in this way; some in others. I myself, at one time, was completely unable to accept a deep depression over the Orkneys. For Brother Stanley it is the wind—

BROTHER CYRIL: *(To his feet again)* Ah, the wind, the wind! The wonderful . . .

BROTHER MERVYN: Sit!
    (Brother Cyril sulks)

BROTHER GREGORY: Er . . . there was one other thing.

ALL: *(Leaning in unison towards him)* Yes?

BROTHER GREGORY: Well, I wondered how you stand on temperature measurement. I know some groups believe you won't get into the meteorological office unless you measure in Centigrade.

SISTER FELICITY: Brother Gregory, we believe that the important thing is to measure temperature. Some of us do measure it in Centigrade. *(Shyly)* I started one morning quite suddenly a few weeks ago; but some people will always measure in Fahrenheit. That doesn't mean they're not Fishites.

BROTHER MERVYN: We do in fact have a small group who meet every Monday evening just to measure temperature in Centigrade. There's no question of a split.

SISTER LAETITIA: We're all quite calm about it.

BROTHER CYRIL: *(Stands: chants wildly)* Brother Giles we stand with you, freezing point is thirty-two! Fahrenheit is always—

ALL: Sit down! Shuddup! Give it a rest! *etc.*

BROTHER MERVYN: Well, Brother Gregory, we now move into the final part of our meeting. Do you wish to stay?

BROTHER GREGORY: Er . . . yes, I suppose so.

BROTHER MERVYN: Very well then. Let us proceed with the ceremony of initiation. Let us stand and affix the blindfolds.

(All stand and put on blindfolds except Brother Gregory)

BROTHER MERVYN: Brother Earnest—if you please!

(Brother Earnest starts his rhythmic tapping on the barometer. They all stand on one leg, extend one hand in front of them, and hop around the stage area hunting for Brother Gregory. As they hop they chant the same words over and over again)

ALL: Seek him! Seek him in the fog! Seek him! Seek him in the fog! *etc.*

(Gregory frantically ducks away from the searching hands, and makes his exit. After a few seconds they too exit, still chanting as they go)

End

The Preacher

I FIRST TOOK an interest in the Christian faith when a young curate, having failed to impress me with rational arguments, lost his temper a little and cried, 'I love him! I just love him! I love Jesus!'

It was the passion in his statement that intrigued me. You can find that same passion in the outpourings of all the biblical characters who walked closely with God. Without this extravagance of feeling towards God, the Christian religion is a very unappealing club. It doesn't have to be expressed in a particular way. Some people use explicit words and movements, others are clearly hugging an immense secret joy within themselves that spills out in love and care for others.

The Preacher was written at a time when this whole issue had become something of a problem to me. In the situation I was in I seemed to see more passion and commitment outside the church than in. I was very arrogant about it—still am probably. The point remains though. Passion pulls people!

The Preacher

The preacher stands, his people's rock,
And prays mid walls of stone,
Oh, let my congregation's doubts
Be greater than my own.

I shall not look at Mrs Cook,
For her salvation's won,
But I shall speak to Rosie Cheek,
The whore of Babylon.

For Rosie will not humble me,
Her sins are rich and red,
And seven devils throng her soul,
So Mrs Cook has said.

Oh, Rosie, do not fail me now,
I need you for a while,
I do not ask that you repent,
If you will only smile.

My curate will not smile at me,
I fear he is devout,
I fear he fears I fear that he
Will shortly find me out.

He is a strong yet humble man,
His words are firm but meek,
He bores me to the depths of hell,
God bless you, Rosie Cheek.

I try to love them all, O Lord,
And preach your holy book,
But faith that can move mountains
Would stop short at Mrs Cook.

The preacher sits. Do angels sing?
Have they now what they seek,
Safe in the arms of endless love,
The soul of Rosie Cheek?

For in the lamplit study now,
The coals are burning low,
As cold salvation freezes fast,
The living waters flow.

O Lord, would she have kept her smile
If she had come to me,
And notwithstanding Mrs Cook,
Be closer now to thee?

Salt of the Earth

Salt of the Earth makes the same point as the last piece. Only an excited appreciation of the way in which Jesus dynamically affects the world can infect others. Books, opinions and theories are no substitute for personal and passionate involvement. It's good to put a bit of welly into this song!

Salt of the Earth

WORDS & MUSIC: ADRIAN PLASS

WORDS BY THE MILLIONS BOOKS BY THE TON

WHAT A LOT OF READING EVERY BODY'S DONE HOW THEY GONNA KNOW WHAT

JESUS IS WORTH WELL I KNOW KNOW

KNOW YES I KNOW HE'S THE SALT OF THE EARTH

JE — SUS JE —

— SUS JESUS IS THE SALT OF THE EARTH

Words by the million, books by the ton,
What a lot of reading everybody's done.
How they gonna know what Jesus is worth?
Well I know, know, know, yes I know he's the salt of the
    earth.
Jesus, Jesus, Jesus is the salt of the earth.

Many people tell me they can only recall
Failure to discover any flavour at all,
I know I'm not exactly spilling over with mirth,
But I know, know, know I know he's the salt of the earth.
Jesus, Jesus, Jesus is the salt of the earth.

Everybody has a little something to say,
You'd think that they were there on resurrection day,
You'd think that they were present at his moment of birth,
But do they know, know, know, do they know he's the
    salt of the earth?
Jesus, Jesus, Jesus is the salt of the earth.

God is in his heaven, is his heaven in you?
Can you hear him saying what he wants you to do?
Jesus is the one and only way to rebirth,
And then you, you, you, yes you will be the salt of the
    earth.
Yes, you, you, you, oh you will be the salt of the earth,
Jesus, Jesus, Jesus is the salt of the earth.

PROMOTE PARTY-SPIRIT!

Hallelujah in the Back of My Mind

I DON'T MIND denominations. In fact, I like them really. It's always good to have a variety of flavours available, and it's not a bad thing to educate your tastebuds with the odd sip at a concoction you've never tried. A local pastor said at a (genuinely) ecumenical meeting recently that if we have real love for each other as followers of Jesus, then we have the only kind of unity that really matters. I think he's right, although that 'if' can be a rather large one sometimes.

From the unchurched person's point of view though, it must all be a bit confusing, especially if he or she encounters one of those church-hopping individuals who is constantly leaving a fellowship or church because of some obscure piece of 'totally unacceptable' dogma, never pausing to reflect that his inability to settle might be something to do with *him*. I think I was a bit like that—over-critical and judgemental. It was a great relief to discover eventually that a simple commitment to one church, and a willingness to accept that church in the same way that God accepts me, was the antidote to that kind of restlessness.

During a period of nearly two years when we didn't attend any church, however, I got pretty fed up with *all* the denominations, and wrote the words of *Hallelujah in the Back of My Mind* as an expression of my frustration. It was also a cry of relief that God stayed with me when the church institutions seemed so uninviting. I can still sing or read the words with real feeling, but I have to add that, in my view, denominational differences can be yet another devilish red herring—or dead kipper.

The message is all in the words, so there's no point in bashing through too quickly. When I read it as verse, I usually leave out all but the final chorus, otherwise it lasts for about three weeks . . . .

The tune is by James Hammond.

51

Hallelujah in the
Back of My Mind

LYRICS: ADRIAN PLASS
MUSIC: JAMES HAMMOND

I take my problems to the altar, but my steps begin to falter,
And I feel as if I'm starting to fall,
For it's hard to recollect the proper way to genuflect,
Upon arrival in a Pentecostal hall.
And I really want to share it but I know they'll never wear it,
And the question in my head is underlined,
But just as I am saying, who on earth invented praying,
Hallelujah in the back of my mind.

Chorus:
    Hallelujah in the back of my mind,
    Hallelujah in the back of my mind,
    I've got to hand it to you, Lord,
    You're really coming through.
    With Hallelujah in the back of my mind.

There are some who have you kneeling, there are those
    who hit the ceiling,
There are others who insist on a smell,
There are some who keep their hats on, and a very few are
    bats on,
Having serpents in the service as well.
There are those who call you 'sinner', if you dare enjoy your
    dinner,
And Gommorrah's in a half a glass of wine,
But just as I am sure I can't survive it any more,
Hallelujah in the back of my mind.

Chorus:
    Hallelujah . . . *etc.*

Well, they say, 'Oh yes you may do what you feel because it's
    real,
And everybody must be perfectly free,
And I'm happy to advise you, not a soul will criticise you,
Just as long as you are copying me.'

So I take it and I shake it and I really try to break it,
And I think I'm gonna leave it behind,
But just as I've dismissed it, there's a sound, I can't resist it,
Hallelujah in the back of my mind.

Chorus:
   Hallelujah . . . *etc.*

There's a man who when I'm sickly, says, 'You very, very quickly
Should be starting to be better, not worse,'
And he tells me that he sees I'm needing longer on my knees,
And there will always be a relevant verse.
But some say if you suffer, then your spirit will get tougher,
So you'd better find a will and get it signed,
But just as I'm refusing to go on, it's so confusing,
Hallelujah in the back of my mind.

Chorus:
   Hallelujah . . . *etc.*

There are many, many people, who rely upon a steeple,
To remind them that they're aiming at God,
While some discover Zion under corrugated iron,
And they none of them believe they are odd,
For they know the congregation in their own denomination
Is the nearest thing to heaven you can find,
But when I say, 'That's it! O Lord, I know I'll never fit,'
Hallelujah in the back of my mind.

Chorus:
   Hallelujah in the back of my mind,
   Hallelujah in the back of my mind,
   I've got to hand it to you, Lord,
   You're really coming through
   With Hallelujah in the back of my mind.

Anagrams

PROBLEMS CAN ARISE from denominational differences when a particular group or church or fellowship seizes on one detail or aspect of religious activity and majors on it to such an extent that the really vital things become relatively unimportant. A man stands under an apple tree. Five apples hit him on the head. As the fifth one strikes he has a divine revelation. Before long 'The Church of the Fifth Apple' is planted. Every Sunday fruit figures heavily in the order of service. A bit of an exaggeration? Well, yes . . . perhaps, but you know what I mean.

Readers of *The Sacred Diary* can't have failed to become aware that I'm a little keen on working out anagrams for the names of famous Christians and politicians. One or two earnest folk have said to me, 'You know, there's more in these anagrams than meets the eye.'—Noting the gleam in their eye that suggests they are about to found the 'Church of the Fifteenth Anagram', I always hasten to assure them that it's just a bit of fun. But those comments set me thinking. What might the equivalent of the Anglican Lesson sound like in the 'Church of the Fifteenth Anagram'?

The piece entitled *Anagrams* hopefully makes the point about undue emphasis, but it's also an opportunity to say one or two serious things in the midst of humour. The 'congregation' can be as small as two, or even one, if volunteers are scarce. I often leave out the response sections and do it as a one-man reading. The voice needs to be that of your average stage vicar, evening out into normal tones for the final more serious sections.

(N.B. There's no reason why people shouldn't add anagrams of their own church leaders to the list, or even substitute more topical politicians as time goes by.)

Anagrams

READER: The first lesson is taken from the second book of Anagrams, chapter five, verse sixteen, beginning at Ronald Reagan. May our names be unchanged!

CONGREGATION: (*in flat unison*) Sock it to us, Julie.

READER: May we never suffer rearrangement!

CONGREGATION: We do not know what you are talking about, Bernard.

READER: May our letters stay intact!

CONGREGATION: If you don't get on with it, Myrtle, we shall come up there and rearrange your liver.

READER: Two Anagrams, chapter five, verse sixteen. And Ronald Reagan was an anagram of 'An oral danger'.
And David Steel was an anagram of 'Vital deeds', and 'Slated dive'.
And David Owen was an anagram of 'An odd view', and 'A dive down', and 'Dawn video'.
And Neil Kinnock was an anagram of 'I knock Lenin'.
And Maggie Thatcher . . .
     (*All kneel*)
was an anagram of 'Get rich team hag'.
And Norman Tebbit was an anagram of 'Ointment barb', and 'Mor'n a bit bent'.
And Enoch Powell was an anagram of 'One we'll chop'.
And Max Bygraves was an anagram of 'Marvy sex-bag'.
And Alvin Stardust was an anagram of 'I trust vandals'.
And Barry Manilow was an anagram of 'Woman Library'.
And love . . .
     (*All stand*)

CONGREGATION: (*like a sighing wind*) Yes . . .?

READER: . . . is an anagram of 'Vole',
And lost love . . .

CONGREGATION: Is an anagram of . . .?

READER: 'Vole slot'.
   (*Boldly*) And Robert Runcie is an anagram of 'C.E. but in error'
   And 'Ice-bun terror'.
   And Billy Graham is an anagram of 'Big rally ham'.
   And mother-in-law is an anagram of 'Woman Hitler'.
   And Mother Theresa is an anagram of 'Heart rest-home'.
      (*Pause*)
   And security is an anagram of 'Rusty ice'.
      (*All take up the sss . . . of 'ice'*)
   And sweat is an anagram of 'Waste',
   And close friend is an anagram of 'Closer fiend'.
   And apartheid is an anagram of 'Death pair'.
READER AND CONGREGATION: 'A dire path'
   'A heart dip'
   'A dirt heap'
READER: A death rip.
   And tomorrow is an anagram of 'Root worm'.
   And today is an anagram of 'Toady'.
   And yesterday . . .
   (*Member of crowd sings*), 'All my troubles seemed so far away . . .'
   (*He is quickly extinguished*)
READER: Yesterday is an anagram of 'A seedy try'.
   And nuclear bomb is an anagram of 'Rub once balm'.
   And utter despair is an anagram of 'Rutted Praise'.
   And Armageddon is an anagram of 'An armed God'.
   Here ends the lesson.
      (*Pause*)
VOICE: Lord, in thy mercy . . .
READER AND CONGREGATION: . . . hear our prayer.

The Well

The Well is a parable, so in the best tradition of parable tellers I shall let it speak for itself.

The Well

Once upon a time a rich landowner built a village and
invited people to come and live in it. He pointed out that a
well had been sunk in the centre of the village square, and
being a good man, he was particularly anxious to make it
clear that each villager, however humble, had an equal right
to draw water at any time and in any quantity he or she
wished, especially as there was no other water source
available. He then set off on his travels, confident that all
would be in harmony when he returned in the distant
future.

For a time the villagers used the well as the landowner
had intended, but gradually things changed. The richer and
more socially prominent citizens began to feel annoyed that
the humbler element in the village were able to keep *them*
waiting in a queue. It didn't seem right. They solved the
problem by creating new village laws about access to the
well. Water could only be obtained at certain set times and
in certain set quantities. Moreover, two long forms had to
be filled in on each occasion, and water was only to be
drawn by a hireling of the rich faction. Not only did this
solve the queue problem, it also deterred the poorer
villagers from applying for water even at the set times. The
forms were very long and complicated. They preferred to
make do on less water. The rich group on the other hand,
being better educated and more highly motivated towards
the written word, were very happy indeed with the
arrangement. The change in the law they justified by
claiming that a document had been discovered written by
the landowner, and instructing them to proceed in this way.

Time passed.

Some years later an intelligent and very vocal young
man announced that he had been elected as a

representative of the poor people of the village in matters pertaining to water. Furthermore, he informed the ruling group, he too had discovered a document written by the landowner, in which it was stated absolutely clearly that it was quite unnecessary to fill in forms to obtain water. Instead, each villager was to perform a certain sequence of dance steps if he or she wanted access to the well. The details of the dance, he claimed, were contained in the document.

They demanded to see his document. He demanded to see theirs. No documents appeared.

Fearing the vocal young man's capacity for inciting rebellion, the rich faction decided to allow the 'dance-step' method of obtaining water for the poorer citizens, while continuing with the form-filling method themselves.

There were now two official drawers of water posted at the well. One inspected forms and supplied water at set times if the forms were completed correctly, the other studied the execution of the prescribed dance and responded accordingly. Newcomers to the village were obliged to adopt one of these methods for obtaining water, as there was no other source. Occasionally, a villager might change from being a form-filler to being a dancer, or the other way round, but not very often.

As the years passed no one could quite remember the origin of these differences, but as it worked reasonably well, it didn't seem to matter. The only problem was that it did get a bit crowded round the well at times.

Eventually, the landowner returned to the village unexpectedly. Coming up to the well, he was greeted by the two official drawers of water, who asked him if he wished to fill in forms or do the dance. Bewildered, he asked them what they meant. They explained that, as far as they knew, the person who built the village in the first place had laid down a law that water was only to be given to dancers or form-fillers. They were hoping, they added, that the owner of the village would return soon, so that they could persuade him to provide a second well. That would make things so much clearer and more convenient.

The landowner wept.

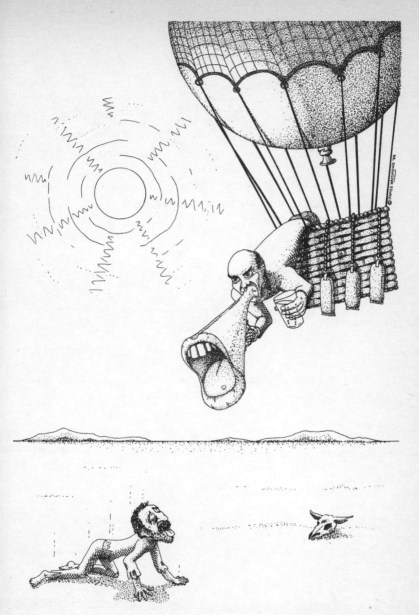

Don't be so apathetic!

MISERY IS
MANIFOLD!

Growbag World

I WROTE *Growbag World* in response to a picture painted by a very close friend of mine. As I sat alone, gazing at his painting of teazles reaching up towards a fragmented moon in an ominously leaden sky, I made rough notes about my immediate reaction to the picture. Later, at home, I wrote a set of verses loosely based on those notes. As the poem progressed, I realised that I was writing more about my friend than about his painting. He is a church leader, an enabler and encourager of others. Over the years thousands of people must have benefited from his consistent warmth and ability to listen without judging and confining. I don't mean that he's flawless. He would laugh at the very idea. I don't think we protect and care for our good church leaders as we should. It's so comfortable to assume that at least *one* person is strong and safe and sound. Actually, the cost of being a public optimist can be enormous. There can be only one hero in the book of any Christian's life, and that's God. The tendency to lean too heavily on individual Christian leaders can be a postponement of real contact with God.

Growbag World

Upon this giant growbag world,
I planted seeds of light,
And dreamed a glowing harvest,
That would penetrate the night.

But as I toiled upon my knees,
They ringed me round with gloom,
Their pockets full of pallid hands,
Their voices full of doom.

'We tell the truth, the truth is dark,
There is no light to save,
Your seeds will never break the earth,
Your garden is a grave.'

And yet I work, I work, I work,
And now my seeds have grown,
I touch the cold and lightless leaves,
And love them as my own.

And will there come a morning soon,
When flowers from the shade,
Will bloom and break, and float, and light
The world that you have made?

How hard, how hard, to paint a dream,
For eyes that cannot shine,
For eyes too dulled by twilight skies,
To see the dawn in mine.

Poison Pools

SIN CAN BE very attractive, especially if the alternatives appear joyless and full of strain. Why try, if trying looks more like gloom than glory? That's how I felt when I wrote *Poison Pools*. I try to remember that feeling now when I meet Christians who are low. Jesus came down to rescue us. Let's go down to rescue our brothers and sisters, then we can climb back up together. Someone did that for me.

Poison Pools

Who made these poison pools
In desert lands
So sweet and cool
A welcome lie
The chance to die with water on my lips
I've seen how others try to die unpoisoned in the sun
I do not think that I can do as they have done.

Shell

As I WRITE I am approaching forty. The last four years of my life have probably been the most satisfying I've known. I'm going to have a big party when I reach my fortieth birthday. I shall expect my guests to bring large expensive presents and bottles of reasonable wine. There has been a lot to thank God for lately.

I hated becoming thirty. I wrote this poem on August the fourth, nineteen seventy-eight. It's how I felt, and I'm glad it's there as a record, or a yardstick, or something. It's a part of my shadow that's better out than in . . .

Shell

Saw a shell
Rich with mother-of-pearl
Waited
So long
To see the creature that needed such delicate protection.
Realised
So late
The creature was long gone
Soaked with sea
Drifting in heaven or hell
But certainly
Not minding.

When Does the Joy Start?

WHY DO SO many Christians ask this question? Like disappointed children they can't understand why the promises don't seem to be kept. Especially, perhaps, they have great difficulty in believing that God really loves *them*. How gratifying for the devil to see how this most basic truth and reassurance is denied to many who want to follow Jesus. Only love will reveal love—not slick answers.

I wrote *When Does the Joy Start?* when I needed answers myself.

When Does the Joy Start?

WORDS & MUSIC: ADRIAN PLASS

The light I have is slowly fading,
There's no sign of a change;
Tell me why is this darkness
So sweet and so strange?
Did I think you were joking?
Did I think you were mad
When you told me to follow
The good and the bad?

When does the joy start?
When do the clouds part?
When does the dawn break?
When does the earth shake?
When does the choir sing?
When do the bells ring?
When will I rise with him?

My friends all say I should be leaving,
It may be true that I'm slow,
If you know me like they do
Do you still want to know?
If I knew where to head for,
I would certainly go;
I need someone to tell me,
And you seem to know.

So when does the joy start?
When do the clouds part?
When does the dawn break?
When does the earth shake?
When does the choir sing?
When do the bells ring?
When will I rise with him?

I shall not move until you bless me,
I will stand by your door,
In your moment of leaving
You will see me, I'm sure.
All I need is a moment,
All I ask is a smile,
Just to know that you love me,
That'll do for a while.

And that's when the joy starts,
That's when the clouds part,
That's when the dawn breaks,
That's when the earth shakes,
That's when the choir sings,
That's when the bells ring,
That's when I rise with him.

That's when you'll see me,
That's when you'll free me,
That's when my star falls,
That's when my God calls,
Calls out to my heart,
That's when the joy starts,
That's when I rise with him.

PERFECTION
IS
POSSIBLE!

The Law

I ONCE MADE a television programme with Peter Ball, the
Bishop of Lewes. As we stood in near darkness at one end of
the studio waiting for the floor manager to call us onto the
set, someone asked Peter how sure he was about some
aspect of Christian doctrine. Dear Peter gives just about
everything he's got in every waking hour, but on this
particular morning he was very low.

'The only thing I'm sure of at the moment,' he said
quietly, 'is that I'm a sinner.'

Fortunately, Peter knows that God is always willing and
able to forgive him. He has practised being forgiven for
years. That doesn't mean it's invariably easy, but it does
mean that, in a very real sense, hope springs eternal.

Most of us can identify with the feeling that our sin is
the only thing we're sure about. The problems come when
forgiveness is not a corresponding or balancing fact of life.
For years I laboured under the delusion that I needed to
earn my way into God's good books. I knew the theology,
but I wasn't convinced. The result was a sort of superficial,
arid virtue, bloodless and boring. Sin continued of course,
but even the sin wasn't very interesting. So many people I
meet are still trying to live according to law. We can't do it.
Jesus died *because* we can't do it. We only have to be
conscious for a few seconds each morning to know that the
law is too much for us. That knowledge, properly
understood, can be the beginning of freedom.

The Law is, again, a simple piece of verse, but it repays
careful rehearsal by the two participants. Wigs and gowns
add a lot, but aren't essential. A fairly sharp contrast
between the personalities of Murgatroyd and Pratt is an aid
to effectiveness. Above all—enjoy it! The two lawyers rather
relish the hopelessness of their message.

The Law

MURGATROYD: We have a feeling some of you
    Are feeling fairly sure
    That all you really need to do
    Is try to keep the law.
PRATT: You wish you knew for sure, though,
    Can you break it once or twice,
    And still get into heaven?
    What you need is some advice.
MURGATROYD: You need some legal expertise,
    And we provide just that,
    We are your humble servants
    Messrs Murgatroyd . . .
PRATT: And Pratt.
MURGATROYD: The law is rather difficult,
PRATT: There's such a lot of it,
MURGATROYD: Perhaps you haven't understood.
PRATT: Perhaps you are a twit.
MURGATROYD: If you decide to live by law
PRATT: You'd better heed our warning,
MURGATROYD: The first mistake that you will make
PRATT: Is waking in the morning.
MURGATROYD: The moment the alarm has gone
PRATT: You'll make a tiny slip,
MURGATROYD: And by the time you're out of bed,
PRATT: You're in the devil's grip!
MURGATROYD: You can't be bad,
PRATT: Or sad
MURGATROYD: Or mad
PRATT: Or rude
MURGATROYD: Or crude
PRATT: Or greedy,
MURGATROYD: You're not allowed to flash

PRATT: Your cash, (*holds up wads of notes*)
MURGATROYD: You give it to the needy. (*Takes cash from Pratt*)
MURGATROYD: You aren't allowed
PRATT: To shun the crowd
MURGATROYD: You've got to love them all,
PRATT: Especially if
MURGATROYD: They bore you stiff
PRATT: And drive you up the wall.
MURGATROYD: You mustn't steal
PRATT: Or fight
MURGATROYD: Or feel
PRATT: Embarrassed by your zits.
MURGATROYD: Or go along to swimming pools
PRATT: To look at naughty bits.
MURGATROYD: Can you forgive your cousin, Viv,
PRATT: And tell her so as well?
MURGATROYD: And stay with ancient Auntie May
PRATT: Despite the horrid smell?
MURGATROYD: And if you're lending anything
PRATT: That you will sadly miss,
MURGATROYD: You're not allowed to want it back,
PRATT: For instance—lend me this! (*Takes back cash*)
MURGATROYD: And if you *do* do something right
PRATT: It's no good saying, 'Well!
PRATT/MURGATROYD: I *am* a little sunbeam now'
MURGATROYD: That's pride,
PRATT: You'll go to hell.
MURGATROYD: We hope we have conveyed to you
PRATT: The danger you are in,
MURGATROYD: But please, you mustn't worry,
PRATT: No you mustn't, it's a sin.
MURGATROYD: You see, you'll never keep the law,

PRATT: There's not a chance of that.

MURGATROYD: We promise you can take the word—of
    Murgatroyd

PRATT: And Pratt.

I Found a Bird

ONE OF THE greatest barriers to prayer in my life has been an obsession with self-image. I never wanted to let God in through the front door of my life until I'd tidied up all the messes, done the washing-up, cleaned the windows and made the beds. Never realising how gladly and joyfully he would have come in, rolled his sleeves up and given me a hand, I kept him waiting outside while I tried to do an impossibly perfect job on my own. Ironically, it wasn't until I hit rock-bottom a few years ago that I realised how all that stuff about God loving me whatever happened was true. In the darkest and most difficult times Jesus was there—sometimes in the most unlikely situations. He wasn't ashamed to be with me, just as he wasn't ashamed to be with publicans and sinners two thousand years ago.

Nowadays, I tend to leave the door on the latch.

I Found a Bird is from those dark days. Best sung without accompaniment if you have the courage. I don't very often.

I Found a Bird

WORDS & MUSIC: ADRIAN PLASS

I found a bird with a broken wing,
When she knew that I loved her,
She began to sing.
Did you ever lose someone?
Have you ever felt blue?
If you ever go down there,
He's there with you.

I know a bar, where my wild time blows,
There's a tune on the juke-box,
Sad as a rose.
Have you ever been down there?
Have you ever been blue?
If you ever go down there,
He's there with you.

Then you find a road, seems to lead somewhere,
They say you'll go a long way
On a wing and a prayer,
But did you ever just wonder,
Why you still feel blue?
If you ever go down there,
He's there with you.

Whoever made days, didn't make them right,
'Cause the days keep changing
Into weeping nights.
Have you ever been lonely?
Have you ever been blue?
If you ever go down there,
He's there with you.

We all gotta change the way that we are,
Every last one of us
Gonna find our star.
But if you ever grow weary,
If you ever just feel blue,
If you ever go down there,
He's there, he'd love to be there, with you.

I Didn't Have to See You

I HAVE A friend called Paul Winter. He's a postman. Very occasionally he comes round with a tune he's worked out on the guitar and invites me to come up with some words to fit the music. I play a tape of his accompaniment over and over again until something vaguely suitable suggests itself. I rather enjoy the process. Because the tune already exists it feels more as if I am discovering the words than creating something new.

I Didn't Have to See You was born by this method, during a period when I was recovering from illness, and it records a growing awareness that the way I feel, physically, emotionally or spiritually has little to do with God's ever-present love and faithfulness. That sounds all very wonderful of course, but I very frequently have a job remembering it. One of his infernal majesty's most effective pieces of rubbish!

I Didn't Have to See You

LYRICS: ADRIAN PLASS
MUSIC: PAUL WINTER

I didn't have to see you
In the night-time, there by the side of me,
I knew it had to be you,
Knew you loved the child inside of me,
You smiled in the darkness,
It seemed to blind and burn,
But when my eyes were opened,
I smiled in return, for you were there.

I didn't have to hear you,
In the silence you were a part of me,
I knew that I was near you,
Knew your love was deep in the heart of me,
I knew that you were saying,
Our happiness has grown,
For prayer is only friendship,
You never were alone, for I was there.

I didn't have to hold you,
I was trusting, knowing your care for me,
The secrets I had told you,
Knowing you would always be there for me,
So let the darkness gather,
And let the silence roll,
The love that made you suffer,
Is glowing in my soul, and you are there.

My Baby

I HAVE TO confess that, as clay goes, I'm not very good at accepting everything the Potter says and does without question. I have often come to a frowning halt while reading Scripture, my twittering finite mind unable to proceed because something God has said or done 'isn't fair', or 'doesn't make sense'. Part of me likes the fact that some questions are unanswerable—one of the best pieces of advice I was ever given was, 'learn to live in the mystery'—but another part of me moans and grunts and huffs at the prospect of simply accepting apparently unacceptable truths. God forgives me, irksome though I am, and even, very occasionally, provides aids to acceptance. *My Baby* is one of those.

When I was working on the narration side of David and Bathsheba (see *Nathan Rap* pre-amble), I came to one of those full stops of non-acceptance when I read about the death of David's son, the baby born out of David's illicit union with Bathsheba. The Bible states quite categorically that God caused the baby to fall sick and die as a specific punishment for David's crimes of adultery and murder. I found myself unable to carry on with the narrative because an overwhelming question blocked the way.

Why? Why did God kill the baby? *How* could he?

Traditional answers were no use to me. I knew them— had used them to answer others. They sprang to mind with Pavlovian ease. None of them allowed me to go on writing. David, I was interested to note, was able to accept the death of his child, not without grief, but without a trace of anger or resentment.

I couldn't accept it.

Then one afternoon, as I was walking the half-mile or so to collect my sons from junior school, a procession of words marched through my brain. When I got home I wrote them down, and soon the narrative was complete. It's not *the* answer. It's *an* answer—my answer, but I think others might find it helpful. One of the devil's most successful deceptions is the one about God standing aloof and detached from human suffering. He knows how it feels, and he shares in it.

My Baby

I wish you knew how much I love you all. I wish you could trust me in the way that David did. You've asked me a question about the death of a baby. Now I will ask *you* some questions, and you must decide whether I've earned the right to be trusted whatever I do. My questions are about Jesus.

When he was dragged from the garden of Gethsemane after a night of agonised prayer and terrible, lonely fear; when he was put on trial simply for being himself, and beaten, and kicked, and jeered at; did I insist that you solve for me the problem of pain? I let you hurt and abuse my son—my baby.

When he hauled himself, bruised and bleeding along the road to his own death, knowing that a single word from him would be enough to make me release him from his burden, did I let you down? No, I let you crush him under the weight of your cross. My son—my baby.

And when the first nail smashed into the palm of his hand, and everything in my father's heart wanted to say to those legions of weeping angels, 'Go! Fight your way through and rescue him. Bring him back where he belongs,' did I abandon you to judgement? No, I let you kill my son—my baby.

And when he had been up on that accursed cross for three long hours, and with every ounce of strength left in his poor suffering body, he screamed at *me*, 'Why have you forsaken me?' did I scream back, 'I haven't! I haven't! It's all just a nightmare—come back, they aren't worth it!'

No, I loved you too much—far too much to do that. I let your sin cut me off from my son—my baby.

And that death, dismal, depressing and horribly unjust as it was—the death of my innocent son, has brought peace and life to millions who've followed that same Jesus, who came back to life, back to his friends, and back to me.

Trust me. When it comes to the death of babies—believe me—I do know what I'm doing.

Why Did He Choose . . .?

IT WAS THROUGH reading Malcolm Muggeridge's comments on the life of Jesus that I came to realise how vividly alive the Son of God was as a human being. Jesus loved nature (referring to natural beauty often in the gospels), people generally, his friends in particular, the cut and thrust of debate and argument, in fact the whole rich business of being alive. There must have been times when he quietly mused over what might have been, if it had been possible to avoid the path of obedience to the cross.

Why Did He Choose . . .?

WORDS & MUSIC : ADRIAN PLASS

WHAT A MOUNTAIN CLIMBER THIS JESUS MIGHT HAVE BEEN

CLIMBING THROUGH THE SHADOWS OF THE SCARI — EST RAV-INE

COMING THROUGH AND RESTING WHERE THE AIR IS COLD AND CLEAN

WHAT A MOUNTAIN CLIMBER THIS JESUS MIGHT HAVE BEEN

CHORUS

SO WHY DID HE CHOOSE DEATH ON A HILL — SIDE

A-GONY UN — DER A MERCILESS SKY

WHEN HE COULD HAVE STAYED HOME COULD HAVE PLAYED WITH THE THUN-

— DER WAS I REALLY THE REA ——— SON

HE DE-CID-ED TO DIE

What a mountain climber this Jesus might have been,
Climbing through the shadows of the scariest ravine,
Coming through and resting where the air is cold and clean,
What a mountain climber this Jesus might have been.

Chorus:
　　So why did he choose death on a hillside,
　　Agony under a merciless sky?
　　When he could have stayed home,
　　Could have played with the thunder,
　　Was I really the reason he decided to die?

What a disco dancer this Jesus might have been,
Moving sweetly on the Galilean disco scene,
Dancing like a fire through the red and gold and green,
What a disco dancer this Jesus might have been.

Chorus:
　　So why . . . *etc.*

What a famous lover this Jesus might have been,
Up there with the others on the giant silver screen,
Showing all the ladies what a kiss could really mean,
What a famous lover this Jesus might have been.

Chorus:
　　So why . . . *etc.*

What a leg-spin bowler this Jesus might have been,
A holy Rowley Jenkins on some Jewish village green,
Curling like a snake, and taking five for seventeen,
What a leg-spin bowler this Jesus might have been.

Chorus:
    So why . . . *etc.*

What a loving father this Jesus might have been,
Walking by his lady with the children in between,
Something in their faces that I have never seen,
What a loving father this Jesus might have been.

Chorus:
    So why . . . *etc.*

Letter to God— and God's Reply

ONE OF THE things that must have been particularly fascinating for those who followed Jesus through his three-year ministry on earth, was the amazing variety and ingenuity of his approach to people and situations. Take healing for instance. One person, a deaf man, is taken to a quiet place outside the city to receive his healing. (There are obvious practical reasons for that of course.) Another, the man with the withered hand, is placed in front of an entire congregation and publicly healed for a completely different set of very good reasons. The disciples must have lived in a state of constant anticipation. Tax paid with a coin found in a fish's mouth, walking on the water, five thousand fed with one packed lunch—what next?

Bearing all this in mind, it seems strange and sad that the church is so frequently found to be unimaginative and stolidly cautious in its approach to most things. For this reason perhaps, I always used to feel a vague sense of guilt about using 'devices' in my own relationship with God. This was greatly eased when one such device produced unexpected results.

I had written a letter to God, a prayer on paper if you like, and I read it out one night on the TVS epilogue programme *Company*. Imagine my surprise, a couple of days later, when I received a reply to my letter in the post, signed 'God'. What follows is the letter and the reply, together with a small but important explanatory footnote.

I often read these letters to groups or congregations, partly because it was an interesting and moving sequence of events, and partly to encourage others to use whatever novel means of prayer or worship might occur to them.

God is accessible, and he does want to hear from us.

Letter to God . . .

Dear God,

First of all, I'm sorry it's so long since I last wrote. I realise that postcards are a bit of a cop-out, but to be honest I've just had too much that I either had to do, or wanted to do, more than settle down and let you know just how things are. I do think about you quite a lot though, and I'm ashamed to say I often pretend to others that I'm in more regular contact with you than I really am.

'Oh yes,' I say, 'God and I are just like that. I don't know what I'd do if he wasn't constantly advising me on everything; and,' I add, 'he's very fond of me of course.'

Actually, that's one of the reasons I've got down to writing to you at last. You see, although I say that to people, and although part of me is sure it's true, sometimes I think I must be round the bend just thinking it. You see, the trouble is—you're not actually here, and every now and then I panic, and everything goes dark and empty, and the life drains out of anything good, and there seem to be only shadows.

I sometimes think back to those telephone conversations we used to have—when I was writing to you every day—do you remember? I used to get really excited waiting for the phone to go. . . .

Why isn't it like that any more?

I suppose what I'm really saying is, despite the fact that I haven't done much to keep in touch lately, I still want to know that you and me are . . . well, that you are still interested in me.

I'd better confess, by the way, that most of those postcards I sent I wrote in advance, and just sent one every now and then.

So . . . I really haven't done very well, have I? And I wouldn't blame you if you didn't answer this letter. In fact, I don't know why you seemed so taken with me in the first place. People I knew said that it was because you didn't really know me, and that I was a 'big-head' to think that you had any time for ordinary people like me. But what they don't know is about all those things I told you about myself—some of them I've never told anyone else. Also, none of them knew how after a long time of nobody speaking, and me thinking you'd put the phone down because you were so disgusted, you said, 'I knew all about that before we met, and it makes no difference.'

And I said, 'Why not?'

And you said, 'Because I love you.'

Well, I suppose I want to get back to the way I felt then, and I've been reading all your old letters over and over again. It's almost like having you here in the room.

Now that I've written properly, please call me—soon.

I'll be waiting to hear from you,

Love,
Adrian

... And God's Reply

Dear Adrian,

I was so glad to receive your letter at last, and to know that you still think about me. I thought this was better than a phone call, and of course I am sending this message through someone whom I trust, and who has great faith. I do hope you have been able to clear your mind in those areas that needed clearing, and I also want to let you know that *I* think of *you* all the time.

There are so many I have to share my love with, and so many find it difficult to express themselves. Others find it easier. I know people have great difficulties in praying, but to me *any* communication is better than nothing. Don't forget, Adrian, that I am always listening—and it's so simple really. Just speak from the heart.

You won't forget to communicate again, will you? I'll look forward to it.

My love is with you always,

God.

NB Close examination of the handwriting revealed that the letter was actually written by my mother. Later I learned that she had been up late one night and seen the broadcast in which I read my letter to God. She felt that God wanted her to convey his reply to me. I believe she was right.

Hall of Mirrors
When I Was a Small Boy

MOST OF MY adult life has been spent working with
disturbed children in a variety of settings. In the process I
probably learned more about myself than anything else, but
some things became clear. For instance, I realised
eventually that most of the children I met in boarding
schools for the maladjusted, assessment centres, and secure
units had one problem in common. They needed to know
who and what they were. It wasn't easy for them because
there was more than one answer available to the question
they were constantly (if unconsciously) asking. It was rather
like standing in one of those halls of distorting mirrors. The
child's own family flung one reflection back at him, the staff
in his residential establishment another, the dreaded 'file'
yet another, and then there were friends, the police
perhaps, one or more sets of foster parents, and his own
social worker, a figure who was supposed to provide
consistency but might actually change with bewildering
frequency.

Hall of Mirrors was a simple and certainly inadequate
expression of this particular problem, but I was interested
much later on, when I left residential social work because of
my own emotional problems, to see how these few lines
summed up the problems I was experiencing with my
spiritual identity. What were the distorting mirrors that
prevented me from seeing God clearly? This book is full of
them.

How about you?

When I Was a Small Boy is a record of my own rather
pessimistic fear that the wounds of childhood can never
really be healed. The poem is now largely out of date, thank
God.

Hall of Mirrors

Stranded in the hall of mirrors
I must struggle to avoid
Images that cannot show me
Something long ago destroyed.

In the darkness, in the distance
In a corner of my mind,
Stands a puzzled child in silence,
Lonely, lost and far behind.

In imagination only,
In my single mirror see,
Clear and calm, the one reflection
Of the person that is me.

When I Was a Small Boy

When I was a small boy in a small school,
With endless legs
And ears that widely proclaimed a head full of emergencies,
When I clung by bleeding fingertips
To thirty-three plus nine,
And cognitive dissonance was a hard sum,
There were only two crimes.
The first was shouting in the corridors,
The second was to be a fool,
And when the bell,
The blessed bell,
Let me fling my body home,
I thought I might, at least, one day, aspire to rule in hell,
But now, I never hear the bell,
And part of me
Will always be
A fool
Screaming, in some sacred corridor.

Nice

THE *Nice* SKETCH is a rather alarmingly raw slice of life. It involves a married couple, well practised in the art of tearing each other to pieces, battling doggedly along one of their familiar argumentative ruts. It has been our experience (I have always performed the sketch with my wife, Bridget) that it touches people and provokes response on a number of levels, especially in the case of married couples. It has no visible Christian content, but I think that's the whole point. Many married Christian couples simply cannot understand why they experience such intense and even violent conflict in a relationship which 'should' be loving and peaceful. This sketch offers no answers, but it might, like a benevolent grenade, explode some of the resistance people quite naturally feel to the idea of opening up to others who might be able to help.

Nice does require some acting skill and careful direction. Ideally it's performed in a pool of light. The only other things required are a suitcase which is being packed with clothes by the man as the sketch proceeds, and a single chair. Don't worry about laughs at the beginning of the sketch. They soon fade!

Nice

Man is packing. Woman is watching.

WOMAN: Why are you going?

MAN: I've had enough.

WOMAN: Enough of what?

MAN: Enough of you.

WOMAN: Enough of me what?

MAN: Enough of you asking me what I've had enough of.

WOMAN: You must have had enough of some *thing*.

(*Pause*)

What have you had enough of?

MAN: Well, if you must know, I've had enough of you being nice.

WOMAN: But what's . . .?

MAN: And loving, and generous, and forgiving, and . . . clean.

WOMAN: What's wrong with being lov—all those things?

MAN: The thing that's wrong with being all those things is that *I'm* not. I'm unpleasant, hateful, mean, unforgiving and scruffy.

WOMAN: No you're not.

MAN: Yes I am.

WOMAN: No you're not.

MAN: (*Loudly*) Yes I am!

WOMAN: Well . . . maybe you are.

MAN: No I'm not!

WOMAN: You just said you were.

MAN: Well, I'm *allowed* to say I am. You're too *nice* to agree with me.

WOMAN: But you just said you didn't like me being nice.

MAN: No I did not.

WOMAN: You did.

MAN: I didn't.

WOMAN: You did!

MAN: I did not. I said I'd had enough of you being nice. I have had sufficient. Thank you for supplying me with an appropriate amount of niceness. I have now had enough. I have packed all your niceness with my socks and shirts and underwear, and I am going to find someone or somewhere that will supply me with an equal amount of something else that I have not got enough of.

WOMAN: It's not fair.

MAN: Thank you for being so understanding.

WOMAN: I meant it's not fair to me.

MAN: But I just told you—I don't do fair things. *You* are fair. *I* am unfair. You are a very wonderful person, I am slightly less wonderful than a turd.

WOMAN: Don't be silly.

MAN: I am also silly.

WOMAN: You're being ridiculous.

MAN: And ridiculous.

WOMAN: What you really mean is that I never give you an excuse for doing the things you've really wanted to do since about two weeks after we got married! You'd like me to be really nasty so that you can storm out and sulk with some sympathetic stray female and moan to her about me not understanding you.

   (*Pause*)

MAN: That's not very nice. That is not very nice at all. I have never, never, ever, ever heard you talk like that before. Never!

   (*Pause*)

WOMAN: Look, I didn't mean *any* of that. It's not true really. I'm sorry. Please forgive me.

MAN: (*She must be joking*) Oh, yes it is! You meant every single word. And *that's* why I'm leaving. Because you think I want you to give me an excuse for doing things that you claim I've really wanted to do since about two weeks after we got married, and that I'd like you to be really nasty so that I can storm out and sulk with some sympathetic stray female and moan to her about you not understanding me. I mean—just how nasty can you get?

(*She cries*)

I even have to do my own packing!

WOMAN: (*Eagerly*) Let me do it for you! I'd like to . . .

MAN: No-o-o thanks. I'd rather do it myself.

(*Pause*)

Very nice of you to offer, though.

Very nice.

WOMAN: But I still don't understand what I've done wrong!

MAN: You've done nothing wrong, that's what you've done wrong. Deliberately, and with malice aforethought, you have set out to do nothing wrong. You are an incurable, incorrigible grown-up, and I am the miserable means by which you train and strengthen the muscles of your horrible maturity. You club me with tolerant wisdom, castrate me with forgiveness, and drown me in *niceness*. You are unmercifully loving. I am getting smaller and smaller and smaller every day. I am running out of ways to bully you or make you sorry for me. I am tired of waiting for you to do something fundamentally mean, or vicious, or disloyal, and I'm not going to wait any longer. I would like to add, though, that throughout everything, you have been unfailingly . . . nice.

(*Pause*)

WOMAN: (*Touches him*) You won't really go. You just wanted to work yourself up so that you could say all that. It's gone now. You won't really go.

(*Long pause*)

MAN: You're absolutely right, of course. I won't really go. I never *do* go, do I? I expect I just—wanted to say all that.

WOMAN: Why don't we just forget about it?

(*Pause*)

I'll unpack for you.

(*Pause*)

Then I'll cook us a nice dinner.

MAN: And you promise you'll try to be just a little nastier?

WOMAN: (*She means it*) I'll do anything that makes you happy, darling. I promise.

MAN: Well, that's very—very nice of you. Very nice.

(*She starts to unpack*)

Stress

STRESS SEEMS TO be one of the diseases of modern living; the emotional equivalent of the common cold. At its worst, though, it's a lot more than that. The whole direction of my life was changed when a severe stress reaction caused me to take early retirement (in my thirties) from work with disturbed children. It has been very satisfying to become involved in a new career, the kind of 'bits and pieces' existence I always craved, but I still experience a build-up of stress from time to time, and it is not pleasant. Fortunately I am, nowadays, aware that a tendency to become stressed is not an indication of spiritual decay, any more than David Watson's depressions were evidence of concealed problems. We are all handicapped, to one extent or another, by aspects of a temperament that we've lugged along behind us all our lives. I wouldn't for one moment wish to discount the possibility of the Holy Spirit healing or changing the negative or wounded parts of us. I know he does. I've seen it and experienced it. I would just like people to appreciate that a physical limp and an emotional handicap are not usually very different. We really do need to look after each other with lots of warmth and not much narrow-eyed insight.

Stress is a fairly light device for excavating this issue, and is best played mainly for laughs until the final verse, which is not very funny.

Stress

I've just been up the doctor's. I said, 'Help me, Doctor
    Brown,'
But he said, 'You've got some tablets!' and he had this awful
    frown,
So I said, 'I've struggled up here from the other side of town,
Because the Downers break me up and then the Uppers get
    me down.'
I'm in a mess,
I'm under stress,
I've *tried* my best to rest without success,
I'm holding it together less and less:
I suffer stress.

Sometimes when I'm feeling very peaceful in my car,
There's some funny little clickings and I know I won't get far
Before the clickings turn to clunkings, and you know what
    clunkings are!
And the garage man will take a look, and frown and say, 'Aha!
Your car's a mess!'
It causes stress,
I've *tried* my best to rest without success,
I'm holding it together less and less:
I suffer stress.

Papers tell you food is bad, avoid the butcher's meat,
The nasty fatty stuff will clog, and knock you off your feet.
Everything is fatal, from meringues to shredded wheat,
If it wasn't for starvation, then I wouldn't dare to eat.
So food's a mess,
It causes stress,
I've *tried* my best to rest without success,
I'm holding it together less and less:
I suffer stress.

The world is full of terrorists who say they've been abused,
They're all against each other, and they're all a bit confused,
Cause they murder little people, and they say when they're
    accused,
'Ah, but if your motivation's right, you have to be excused.'
It's just a mess,
It causes stress,
I've *tried* my best to rest without success,
I'm holding it together less and less:
I suffer stress.

There's weapons pointing east and west, they'll soon be
    flying past,
And I can't sleep for thinking that the end's approaching
    fast,
Every nerve is strained as I await the nuclear blast,
Still—the night they drop the bomb, I 'spose I'll get some
    sleep at last,
But what a mess,
It causes stress,
I've *tried* my best to rest without success,
I'm holding it together less and less:
I suffer stress.

I need a friend to talk to, but they're few and far between,
I ring them up and ask them, but they don't seem very keen,
I'm just as sane as they are, and I never make a scene,
They say I'm too neurotic, but *I don't know what they mean!*
Oh, what a mess!
It causes stress,
I've *tried* my best to rest without success,
I'm holding it together less and less:
I suffer stress.

There Won't Be Time Tonight

There Won't Be Time Tonight is another Paul Winter/ Adrian Plass collaboration. Paul came and recorded the guitar accompaniment and tune one morning, and I spent the whole day obsessively cobbling together words to go with it. The song is about loneliness and the difficulty of expressing feelings. I've heard preachers saying that if you are walking properly with the Lord, you need never be lonely. I suppose they *could* be right. I can't help remembering how much Jesus needed his friends to stay awake and supportive at Gethsemane. I think we probably all need somebody.

We have found that this song is particularly poignant when it follows immediately after the *Stress* poem.

There Won't Be Time Tonight

LYRICS: ADRIAN PLASS
MUSIC: PAUL WINTER

Do you ever go to bed; everyone needs a friend,
Feeling rather low, you need one,
Do you ever lie awake, wishing the night away,
Telling yourself that soon, you'll make one?

Chorus:
    But there won't be time tonight,
    And I don't know how to try,
    No one ever showed me how
    Feelings are meant to fly;
    Every night I go to bed, wishing I had a friend,
    Everyone needs a friend, everyone needs to know
    There is love.

Do you ever walk alone; tell me who made the sky,
Feeling rather strange; where is he?
Do you ever stand and say, maybe he touched my hand?
Maybe one day I'll say, I love him.

Chorus:
    But there won't . . . *etc.*

Do you ever fear your day, how can it be so long?
Terrible fighting on; why should you?
Hard to find a reason for moving towards the night,
Needing to hear a friend say, thank you.

Chorus:
    But there won't . . . *etc.*

MARVELLOUS
ME!

Phone Call

Phone Call needs very little explanation or comment. Most of us, at one time or another, have thrown ourselves into Martha-like activities in order to avoid the personal, intimate, and more deeply demanding relationship that Mary opted for. Having said that, it's worth bearing in mind that Mary probably worked just as hard as Martha when Jesus wasn't actually around.

Busyness usually looks very convincing, but unless its roots are in relationship, it's just another piece of rubbish.

Props? A small table and a telephone. The caller should be making his/her call as an afterthought just before going out.

Phone Call

(Picks up phone and dials a number)

Oh, Jesus—Don't come round tonight,
I'm busy at the hall,
And the chances of a chat with you
Are really rather small.
So many people need me,
And I can't deny them all,
So! It looks as if I won't be in,
If you decide to call.

Yes, Tuesday would be better,
But I think the man next door
Is looking very troubled,
And I've helped him out before.
Well—a friend in need is something
I can never quite ignore,
No—don't come round tomorrow night,
You understand, I'm sure.

(Looks at diary)

Wednesday night? That's study group,
Thursday I'm away,
On Friday I've got tickets
For the local Christian play.
Saturday's the mission,
And that'll take *all* day,
Better if we leave it now
Till Sunday night; okay?

(Pause—nearly replaces receiver. Changes mind)

Oh, Jesus? Do you love me?
Will you ever set me free?
I've built myself a prison,
I've thrown away the key.
I'm weeping in the darkness,
Yes, I'm longing now to see
The plans you have for both of us.
Please come and visit me.

Shoes

WHEN I FIRST met Bridget, my wife, I had only one pair of shoes. Both had large holes in the soles. I have to record that, although I would have defended my faith militantly in all sorts of awkward situations, I was too self-conscious to take communion in an Anglican church. I couldn't bear the thought of everyone seeing the state of my footwear as I knelt at the communion rail. Funny, fickle people we are sometimes. Anyway—that's where the idea for *Shoes* came from. I hope it makes the point that even the most spiritual-*looking* problem can have a very practical cause, and we should never jump to conclusions. Heaven preserve us from people who think they know without asking!

All this sketch needs is a pair of telephones, one of which can be rung if possible. Ted's anger mounts slowly but perceptibly as the conversation proceeds. His final line must be heard *very* clearly.

Shoes

Richard dials a number. Ted's phone rings. He picks it up. Richard speaks.

RICHARD: Hello! Ted?

TED: Ted here, yes. Who's that?

RICHARD: Richard here, Ted. Richard Bellbrook. Hi!

TED: Oh, yes, hello, Richard. What can I do for you? I'm a bit—

RICHARD: Ted, can I speak to you as a friend rather than as a minister?

TED: I don't know, Richard. Have a go and see.

RICHARD: Ha, ha! Very good, Ted, very good. Seriously though, I just rang on the off-chance to have a friendly chat and see how you are. See how you're getting along. Catch up on the old news. Find out how the cookie's crumbling at your end of the packet. No special reason for calling. Just a friendly er . . . call.

TED: Oh, right, fine.
   (*Pause*)

RICHARD: So er . . . how are you?

TED: Fine, Richard. I'm fine thanks.

RICHARD: Good! Good! Wife okay?

TED: Fine.

RICHARD: Kids?

TED: Fine.

RICHARD: Work?

TED: Work's fine.

RICHARD: Car going all right?

TED: Bike. Had to sell the car when—

RICHARD: Bike going okay?

TED: Pedalling along nicely, thanks.

RICHARD: Any golf lately? Haven't seen you up there recently.

TED: Can't afford it, Richard, not since I lost—

RICHARD: Surviving without it, eh?

TED: Oh, fine!

RICHARD: Good, good! So overall you're . . .

TED: Fine, Richard. Overall, I'm just fine.

RICHARD: Good! Great! Wonderful! Marvellous! (*Pause*) Fine.
(*Pause*)

TED: Was that all, Richard, because I really ought to—

RICHARD: Saw you in church on Sunday, Ted.

TED: And I saw you, Richard.

RICHARD: Did you? Yes! Good! So we were er . . . both there
then?

TED: Looks that way, Richard, yep!

RICHARD: (*Casually*) Didn't see you up at the communion rail
though, Ted.
(*Pause*)

RICHARD: No sign of you kneeling up at the er . . .
communion rail to take er . . . communion.
(*Pause*)
No er . . . bread or wine for you this Sunday then?

TED: That's right, Richard.

RICHARD: Nor the Sunday before that, I seem to recall.

TED: Nope!

RICHARD: Nor the Sunday before *that*, Ted.

TED: Nor the Sunday before *that*, if you must know, Richard.

RICHARD: Ted, if you're having trouble at home, I'm sure it
can be sorted out. I'm more than happy to come and talk
it through with you. Getting angry with the wife? Evil
thoughts? Not pulling your weight in the home? Adultery?
Shouting at the kids? Some little private sin? Gay?

TED: Richard, it's not—

RICHARD: There is absolutely no reason why you shouldn't

kneel at that communion rail like anyone else. If you've
got the time I've got the ministry, and though I say it
myself, I do have a bit of a special gift when it comes to
leading lost brothers and sisters through confession to
repentance. Now speak up, Ted. You can't shock me. It
doesn't matter what it is. Covetousness? Theft? Been
dabbling in the occult?

TED: For goodness—

RICHARD: Drink? Drugs? Unbelief? Come on, Ted. What is it
that's preventing you from kneeling at that rail? Cheating
on tax? Sexual perversion? Spirit of criticism? What's
keeping you in your seat on Sunday mornings? Greed?
Spiritual pride? Idolatry?

TED: Don't be ridiculous! It's just—

RICHARD: Are we Christian brothers, Ted?

TED: Yes, but—

RICHARD: Do we trust each other?

TED: Yes, but—

RICHARD: Is there anything you'd keep from me?

TED: No, but it's—

RICHARD: So what's the problem, Bro? Open up and—

TED: (*through bared teeth*) Don't call me Bro!

RICHARD: Open up and share the problem, Ted! I've watched
you every Sunday looking troubled when it comes to the
time for communion, and I know – I just *know*, brother—
that something is preventing you from standing up,
walking down the centre aisle of our church, and
kneeling to receive a blessing, and I feel led to counsel
you now that the time has come to reveal your secret sin
and find freedom!

TED: I haven't got a secret sin! It's just—

RICHARD: (*shouts*) Now is the time for courage, Ted! Gird your

loins and make your mind up that you can and will
unburden yourself! He will not strive for ever, and this is
the acceptable day! Tell me why you cannot kneel at that
communion rail!

TED: You pinhead! It's just—

RICHARD: *Tell* me why you cannot kneel at that communion
rail!

TED: I don't see—

RICHARD: *Tell me why you cannot kneel at that communion rail!*

TED: It's none of your—

RICHARD: *Why can't you kneel at that communion rail?*

TED: *Because I've got holes in my shoes!!*
   (*Slams down phone*)

Operation

Operation is an improvisation that aims to demonstrate the way in which we sometimes trample over God's expert work in the problems and difficulties of our lives. It's so easy to think that we know best, especially perhaps when it comes to timing.

Operation

Ideally, *Operation* involves one adult, who plays the surgeon, and six or seven children who are nurses standing around the operating table. One more child is needed to be the prostrate 'patient'.

The scene opens with the nurses standing silently and attentively around the table as the surgeon, with intense concentration, does something to the side of the patient that is invisible to the audience. For quite a long time the only sound to be heard is an occasional curt request for a scalpel or a swab, instantly and respectfully supplied by the nurses. Children greatly enjoy the challenge of creating the tense stillness of this scene, once they understand how essential it is as a contrast to the disintegration that follows. At last, one of the nurses shows an infinitesimal hesitation in passing an instrument, but her hint of a query is instantly quashed by the surgeon, who impatiently demands the thing he's asked for and returns to his task.

From this point onwards anarchy grows, but to be really effective it must happen *very* gradually. Eventually all the nurses are arguing loudly and aggressively with the surgeon and each other, so violently in fact, that the surgeon is pushed out altogether and drifts away out of sight. The noise is hushed once more when the patient suddenly sits upright, looks at the operation site and says, 'That's not right!' The babble then continues with various improbable 'bits' being removed from the patient and thrown aside by the nurses until someone shouts, 'Hey!—he's dead!' and all exit, still arguing about what *should* have been done.

Operation is extremely effective as long as the need for total concentration and very gradual build-up has been understood and practised a few times.

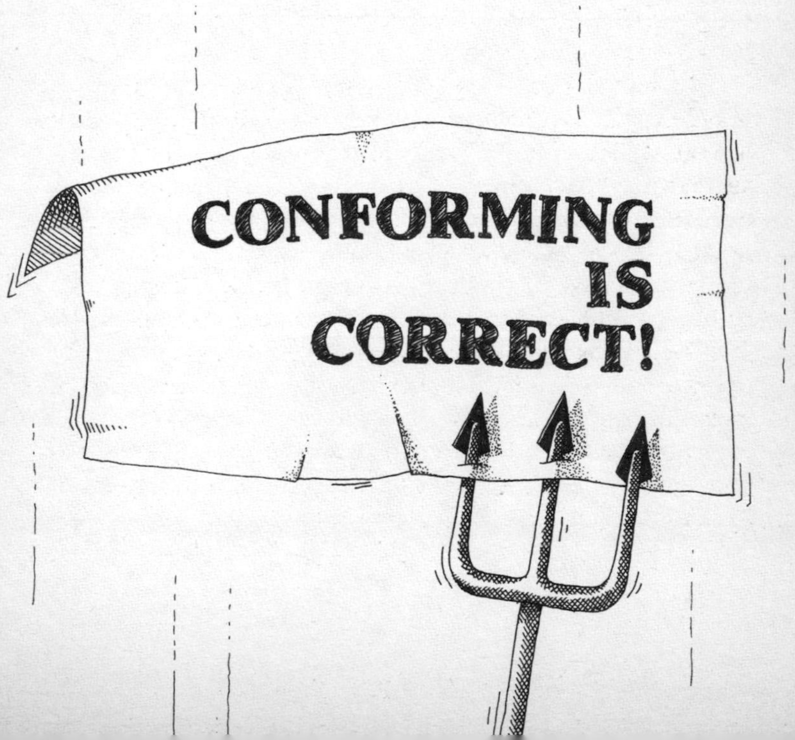
CONFORMING
IS
CORRECT!

The Real Problem

I WAS A rather troubled little boy. Things confused me. I remember feeling particularly anxious about the difference between the way my father was in church every Sunday, and his behaviour at home before and after the service. The hour that we spent in the little Roman Catholic chapel at the end of the village was, all too frequently, sandwiched between much longer periods of anger and tumult. I found it difficult to understand how Dad could switch so easily into a smiling civilised mode, purely, it seemed to me, for the benefit of church acquaintances who never had to witness the scenes of domestic tension and conflict that sprang so easily from his profound insecurity. I wondered why God didn't sort it out. I knew I would have done if I'd been omnipotent.

Nowadays, with three sons under fourteen and a baby daughter who's nearly a year old, it still requires something akin to a small civil war to get everyone clean and dressed and actually moving towards the family service in our local Anglican church. Threats are hissed, small indignant faces are washed, coats are unearthed, the dog, who has tried to follow us, is taken back and incarcerated, and we are on our way at last, usually in a less than holy frame of mind. The difference between my children's experience of Sunday mornings and my own early memories is, I hope, that as a family we are much more honest with ourselves and outsiders than my father ever felt able to be. Thank God for that. Some still aren't able to be that honest.

The Real Problem is a simple little poem, expressing this particular problem from the child's point of view. I usually adopt a childlike tone when performing it, but it isn't really essential. The point is in the words. It is usually received with a low hum of identification . . .

The Real Problem

Sunday is a funny day,
It starts with lots of noise.
Mummy rushes round with socks,
And Daddy shouts, 'You boys!'

Then Mummy says, 'Now don't blame them,
You know you're just as bad,
You've only just got out of bed,
It really makes me mad!'

My mummy is a Christian,
My daddy is as well,
My mummy says 'Oh, heavens!'
My daddy says 'Oh, hell!'

And when we get to church at last,
It's really very strange,
Cos Mum and Dad stop arguing,
And suddenly they change.

At church my mum and dad are friends,
They get on very well,
But no one knows they've had a row,
And I'm not gonna tell.

People often come to them,
Because they seem so nice,
And Mum and Dad are very pleased
To give them some advice.

They tell them Christian freedom
Is worth an awful lot,
But I don't know what freedom means,
If freedom's what they've got.

Daddy loves the meetings,
He's always at them all,
He's learning how to understand
The letters of St Paul.

But Mummy says, 'I'm stuck at home
To lead my Christian life,
It's just as well for blinkin' Paul
He didn't have a wife.'

I once heard my mummy say
She'd walk out of his life,
I once heard Daddy say to her
He'd picked a rotten wife.

They really love each other,
I really think they do.
I think the people in the church
Would help them—if they knew.

Legs

ALL MY LIFE I have bobbed and ducked and weaved to avoid losing my dignity. What a waste of time! I think I've probably learned more through my really idiotic moments than through any amount of supposed cleverness. The more we share failures and weaknesses with others, the more we seem to gain in a different kind of dignity that has nothing to do with vanity or conceit.

The *Legs* incident, which made me feel a first class twit at the time, happened a few years ago, and resulted in me asking myself a question that has seemed increasingly important recently—as I've met so many different people in so many different types of church. When you come to the end of the article (first published in *The Christian Holiday Guide 1988*), do ask the question with me and see if it applies to you, or whether it might apply to people in your church—people who wish they'd had the courage to say how they felt right at the beginning, and fear that it may be too late now.

Legs

Each time we go on holiday I seem to learn one lesson. That's a lot for me.

Like the time when my wife Bridget and I travelled on the coach from Victoria to Norwich. We were excited about going away for a couple of weeks but there was one small problem. My legs are quite long, and unless I sit in one of the front seats in a coach I get most uncomfortable after a short distance.

So we queued for a very long time, at a very early hour of the morning; it was tedious, but I knew it would be worth it.

Then, at the last moment, a woman nipped in ahead of us and grabbed the places we wanted. My wife displayed the kind of righteous aggression that is peculiar to people who are basically kind by nature.

'Excuse me!' she rapped. 'We've queued for these seats for a long time. My husband needs to sit here because of his legs.' The woman moved. She might have argued the point but Bridget's words had provoked a barrage of sympathetic comments from several old dears in the queue behind us.

'Poor dear . . .'

'What a shame . . .'

'E's got bad legs . . .'

'So young . . .'

'Ard for 'is wife . . .'

'Yeees . . . poor soul.'

As our journey began, I sat rather stiffly and self-consciously, aware of several pairs of eyes studying my grey corduroy trousers, picturing with compassionate relish the awful putrefaction that they probably concealed. I hardly noticed the scenery.

The discussion on bad legs in general, and mine in

particular, continued until we stopped halfway through our journey for refreshments at a road-side cafe. We were the last to get off.

As I stepped down I noticed my little support group hovering outside the cafe, watching with barely concealed fascination to see how the badness in my lower limbs would manifest itself when I actually walked.

I know that their expectations shouldn't have influenced me. I *know* that, but I couldn't help it. You would have been strong. I was weak. The dreadful truth is that I limped heavily and artistically from the coach to the cafe with Bridget laughing hysterically beside me.

Ten minutes later I felt obliged to repeat my Hunchback of Notre Dame impression on the return journey, still accompanied by my spluttering spouse. There was no doubt about the impact on my audience. They were very impressed. Not only did this poor man suffer terribly with his decaying nether regions, but he had to contend with a mentally unbalanced wife as well.

Newly inspired, they embarked on a much deeper and more wide-ranging medical discussion as the coach set off once more, a discussion that was still deep into obstetrics as we arrived at the coach station in Norwich.

I haven't got bad legs.
I don't limp.
My wife is quite sane.

What was the question I asked myself as a result of this absurd incident? It was this. How many other small, unreal worlds can be created by misunderstanding and maintained by cowardice. It can happen anywhere. In a coach, or a family, or a church.

God Says

IT CAN BE very tempting to join a group or movement because it offers types of expression and behaviour that are a pleasure to conform to. That may be right. There's nothing wrong with pleasure. But if the springs of liveliness, or liturgical soundness, or silence, or musical excellence, or whatever a particular group offers, are polluted or impure at source, then involvement can be very costly in the long run. It pays to take time and trouble checking that a superficial attraction has the right kind of substance beneath it.

God Says is a piece of buffoonery that makes this point in dramatic fashion. It's probably best used as a means of illustrating or emphasising a point in the course of a presentation or talk, rather than in isolation. Points to remember are that the 'evangelist' must keep his smile on his face *all* through the piece, the crowd must *gradually* respond to his overtures, and their reaction to the shooting must be realistic. By the way, cap guns just aren't loud enough. Get hold of a starting pistol if you can.

God Says

*An evangelist type (probably with American accent) jumps up
onto a chair or table top and addresses the crowd loudly and
aggressively. A fixed grin is plastered over his face throughout all
the proceedings.*

EVANGELIST: Ladies and gentlemen, I am here to tell you that
church does not have to be dull and boring! Church can
be exciting! Church can be fun! Church can be alive and
lively! Where I come from we are never bored in church.
Why are we never bored in church? Because we are in
accord! Why are we in accord? Because everyone in our
church agrees with what I say! I don't know why, but they
do! Hallelujah?
(Crowd responds with unconvinced, muttered Hallelujahs.)
Where I come from we play a game in church! Yes, we
do—we play a game! Brothers and sisters, I sense that
you want to know what that game is! Amen?
(A stirring of interest in the crowd. A few Amens.)
Hallelujah! You shall know because I am going to tell you!
Amen?
(Quite loud Amens from crowd.)
Hallelujah?

CROWD: Hallelujah!

EVANGELIST: Okay! Hallelujah! Over in this country you have a
game called Simon Says. Amen?

CROWD: Amen!

EVANGELIST: Hallelujah?

CROWD: Hallelujah!

EVANGELIST: Well, in the church I come from we play a game
like that, only it's not called Simon Says, it's called God
Says! Amen?

CROWD: Amen! *(Really involved now.)*

EVANGELIST: Hallelujah?

CROWD: Hallelujah!

EVANGELIST: Amen?

CROWD: Amen!

EVANGELIST: God Says is an easy game to play! Every time I say God says do something, you have to do it! But if God doesn't say do it, why then you don't do it! Hallelujah?

CROWD: Hallelujah!

EVANGELIST: Amen?

CROWD: Amen!

EVANGELIST: Hallelujah?

CROWD: Hallelujah!

EVANGELIST: Amen?

CROWD: Amen!

EVANGELIST: *Amen?*

CROWD: *Amen! Hallelujah!*

EVANGELIST: Shall we play the game? Amen?

CROWD: Amen!

EVANGELIST: *Hallelujah?*

CROWD: *Hallelujah! Amen!*

EVANGELIST: (*with a strong swinging rhythm*) God says put your hands on your head!

CROWD: (*Repeating his words and rhythm exactly, performing the required action as they do so. The 'evangelist' repeats the words and performs the actions with the crowd.*) God says put your hands on your head!

EVANGELIST: God says put your hands on your knees!

CROWD: God says put your hands on your knees!

EVANGELIST: God says put your hands on your chest!

CROWD: (*very excited by now*) God says put your hands on your chest!

EVANGELIST: God says put your hands on your ears!

CROWD: God says put your hands on your ears!

EVANGELIST: God says put your hands in your pockets!

CROWD: God says put your hands in your pockets!

EVANGELIST: Put your hands in the air!

(One crowd member puts his hands in the air. The evangelist takes a pistol from his pocket and shoots him. He collapses, moaning and clutching his chest. The crowd gathers round him chilled and shocked.)

PERSON A: You shot him! You just shot him!

EVANGELIST: Well, he shouldn't put his hands in the air when God didn't *tell* him to put his hands in the air! In this game we only do what God says!

PERSON B: But you can't shoot someone just because—

EVANGELIST: Make way there now! *(He comes through the crowd to the injured person, and speaks to him, still pointing his gun.)* Get up now, you're coming with me! *(The injured one cringes back, and the crowd move as if to close in on the evangelist, but he waves them back with his gun.)* GOD SAYS get up now, you're coming with me! *(The injured one hurriedly gets up and goes, followed by the evangelist, still pointing his gun.)* I told you church needn't be boring! Amen?

(The crowd rumbles and boos as he leaves.)

PERSON A: *(shouting after the evangelist very loudly)* You can't shoot someone just because they don't play your game properly!

Neither do I condemn you.

My Way

ONE OF THE games we play in the church is about lifestyle. We are very good at kidding ourselves into believing that religious activities equal Christian living. This applies just as much in new, informal churches as it does in the traditional denominations. I have encountered folk who are feverishly concerned to get 'the worship' right, but never seem to step off the circle line of Bible studies, prayer meetings and Sunday worship to expose themselves to the world that awaits Jesus. Meanwhile, their personal lifestyle remains virtually unchanged. I'm always very wary about reading the gospels. They challenge the way I live in a gritty, practical way. Ask people I don't like to dinner? Love my enemies? Seek the kingdom of God *first*? Be honest about the way I really am? Take the lowest place?—the list is formidable. I can't manage it all, but I am convinced that one of the most dangerous fallacies around is the one that says our social and financial lives can remain safe and unchanged if we seriously intend to follow Jesus.

My Way is a rather absurd re-write of the famous Sinatra song, portraying the pathetically commonplace lifestyle of someone who clearly sees himself as being quite a 'man'. Each line is ludicrously overlength for the tune, and most are best delivered in a flat, rather tuneless voice (not difficult for me). I nearly always 'sing' the song without accompaniment, unless a magician like Chris Norton is around. He amazed me at Royal Week one year by carrying my faltering tones effortlessly and faultlessly through *My Way* without a single rehearsal.

You can get a bit fed up with performing the same things over and over again, but *My Way* still makes *me* laugh.

My Way

Born, yes I was born, at the Gooseberry Bush Nursing
    Home, Farley Road in Thurston, on my birthday, which
    just happened to be a Friday,
And my mother, who has a quite extraordinary memory for
    weather, tells me that it was an exceptionally dry day.
Apparently I was a really independent little devil even then,
    so all the people who saw me at the time say,
When I was supposed to be going to sleep I used to make a
    real old squeaky noise whenever I wanted my way.

School, I went like everyone else, but I didn't do very well
    there, but it wasn't my fault, it was because they made me
    sit next to a kid called Vernon Myres.
But in the end I did get one exam, I got CSE mode 3, grade
    6, in changing tyres,
And I once made a sort of modern art thing, by accident, in
    metalwork, that my mother thought was really good, it
    was a sort of ball of metal with like long thin wires,
But more, much more than this, I made a fruit bowl.

Refrain:
    For what is a man? What has he got? If he's not got a
    reasonable income and some savings in the building
    society, and a membership card for the squash club, and
    a couple of mates to go out with once a week, with the
    wife's say-so, although we do almost get up to some real
    naughties sometimes, he's not got a lot,
    I've got all these now, by careful use of available
    resources, and I did it my way.

Girls, I've had a few, well, one, and I married her, and her
    name's Gloria, and she's a bit taller than me, but it doesn't
    matter,

'Cause I've got this really cool pair of high-heeled cowboy boots, and I make sure all her shoes are very much flatter,
I've tried to get her to walk in the gutter, while I walk up on the pavement, but it's taken a good three weeks of persuasion drat 'er,
But after I'd pointed out that all good relationships depend on compromise, and that I'd smack her in the mouth if she didn't do what she was told, she saw it my way.

Job, I've got a job, at an insurance company, where I do rather important things connected with computers.
And every Friday at lunchtime me and some of the lads go down to the Ferret's Armpit to have more than a couple of Mackeson and orange juices,
We might, also, have a game or two of pool, if anyone's got some 10p's and there aren't any rough people in the public bar who might boot us—off,
And none of us think our boss is any good but we don't say so in front of him, although we're not scared of him; he'd better not get in my way.

Refrain:
For what is a man? What has he got? If he's not got a spirit of adventure like me that leads me to choose a different south coast holiday resort every five years despite Gloria's opposition, and I once got fairly firm with a waiter who was a bit slow with the main course although I don't think he actually heard me because I said it very quietly, then he's not got a lot, I've got a Metro, I hope to move to Surrey one day,
and I'll do it my way.
(*Quietly*) If Gloria agrees.

Machine

Machine IS AN improvisation illustrating very simply that the development of complex structures does not bring about change in individuals, and can in fact be dangerous in the long run to those who attempt to create and control them.

Machine

A mad professor type decides to build a machine. His raw materials are ten robotic human beings who are stacked carelessly in a corner, perhaps moving or stirring randomly. He brings them out two by two, and after adjusting their 'controls', places them in the position where they will perform as machine parts, probably facing each other. After establishing and testing the movements of each pair, he turns them off and brings on the next pair with whom he repeats the process.

Eventually the machine, two lines of people facing each other, is complete. The big moment has arrived. With a bang and a puff of smoke he switches on at the mains, and the machine goes into action. Delighted with his creation, he goes a little too close and drops his glasses into one end of the machine. In his attempt to recover them, he is swallowed up by the machine, and horribly 'digested' by the rows of moving parts. Eventually, his lifeless body is passed back along the machine and thrown out at the point where he fell in. The machine is exultant. Each part can separate and roam the stage, still performing its individual movement until the music stops and all are still.

This exercise can provide a lot of fun in the planning and execution. The selection or recording of suitable machine-like music is an interesting business as well.

N.B. This is not a Plass original! I took part in this exercise years ago when Diana Edwards ran the West Kent Theatre Workshop.

Party and the Dream of Being Special

Party . . .

Some time ago we were faced with the problem of creating a lively party atmosphere on stage. Why a problem? Well, there were only five of us on stage, five characters who were involved in a search for some kind of truth. We solved the party problem in the end by realising that five people talking continuously and simultaneously, is the equivalent of five groups of, say, five or six folk, with only one person at a time speaking in each group. But what should we say? We decided in the end to give each character a short speech which would be repeated over and over again in a variety of tones. The speeches were as follows:

(a) Oh, it's absolutely marvellous! It's absolutely wonderful! He didn't? Oh, he did! What a scream!

(b) Completely unexpected—absolutely unanimous apparently. Didn't know I was so popular. Can't let 'em down of course.

(c) Oh, do you really think so? I'm sure you don't mean it. No one's ever said that to me before!

(d) What an extraordinary coincidence! You're not going to believe this, sweetheart, but that is *exactly* how I feel!

(e) Frankly, a car's a car to me. Just a thing to get me from A to B. Fact that it's a roller is neither here nor there.

With a bit of glass chinking and some fairly manic party-type movements, the resultant babble was extraordinary! It's a device worth remembering for any simulated crowd scene. It doesn't actually matter what the characters say, as long as they vary the tone, *don't stop talking,* and address as many people per second as possible.

The party in our stage show was supposed to be an attempt by five characters to find distraction. One by one they slowed their frenzied speech and movement until the group was just a dejected huddle. Each person then sang a verse of *The Dream of Being Special,* a song about the ways in which people seek satisfaction from the world, but ultimately find disappointment and lack of fulfilment.

Although it was presented as a song originally, I often read it as a poem. These verses concern items of 'rubbish' that people often find very difficult to dispose of.

. . . And the Dream of Being Special

And in the summer sunshine
You believed the things they told you
For it's part of being little
And the trust is right inside you
Like a ball of summer sunshine
In the middle of your body
And you think that it will never
Fade away
But as the days go flying
You are troubled by the shadows
In the hearts and hands and faces
Of the people you had trusted
When they promised you the sunshine
For you hear the winter now
In what they say
And the dream of being special floats away
And the whole damn thing looks so grey.

And how you'd love to picture
The perfection of your lover
Who would be so strong and gentle
That his love would touch your spirit
Through your mind and heart and body
And his tenderness would promise
That the joy of every day
Would be the same
Then one day you feel frightened
When a man who seemed to like you
Puts his hands upon your shoulders
And he holds you far too tightly
And he wants to know your age
But not your name
And the dream of being special floats away
And the whole damn thing looks so grey.

There's a friend you meet on Fridays
He's the one who really knows you
And you tell him you're not suited
To the job that you are doing
But you drink and say don't worry
For I'm planning something different
And I've just about decided
On a scheme
And won't it be electric
When I start my great adventure
And the talent I've been hiding
Has a chance to be discovered
Then you see your friend is smiling
As he smiles every Friday
At your dream
And the dream of being special floats away
And the whole damn thing looks so grey.

And parties they're just places
Where you lean against the doorway
Of the kitchen talking nonsense
To a girl with perfect manners
But you see her eyes are glazing
And you know she's only waiting
For the slightest little chance to
Get away
So then you fill your glass up
As you nurse your tired passion
And remember all the failures
And you wish to God you hadn't
Overfed your fat opinions
With the food your heart was needing
Every day
And the dream of being special floats away
And the whole damn thing looks so grey.

And good old Eammon Andrews
Would come smiling round the corner
With a big red book and people
Who would say 'We always loved you'
And you'd wonder why the hell they
Never told you when you needed
All the love that they could offer
What a shame
But as he moved towards you
You would know it doesn't matter
And it's just another way to
Lose the game that you are playing
For in letters that are golden
On the big red book he'd show you
There is someone else's name
And the dream of being special floats away
And the whole damn thing looks so grey.

When I Became a Christian

I HAD A very definite conversion experience back in the sixties. By that I mean that a sudden vivid awareness of the reality and attractiveness of Jesus caused me to change my mind about the direction in which I wanted to go. The problem after that was that I, in common with many other converts in that period, never really appreciated that there is a difference between conversion and discipleship. As Bob Gordon so usefully puts it, conversion is a change of mind, but discipleship involves a change of life. Perhaps the missing ingredient in the teaching of that decade was the bit about *cost*. I was interested to read somewhere that Billy Graham, when asked if he would like to have changed any aspect of his earlier teaching, replied that he would have been much more emphatic about the total demands of God on any Christian who wanted to see real power in his life. The 'happy ever after' mythology that still bedevils some areas of the church is a particularly subtle means of obscuring a truth that Jesus was absolutely open about. The Christian life is tough, and if it's to be of any real use, demands complete giving of oneself. That's why it's so important that our joy should be full, presumably.

When I Became a Christian started its life as a few scribbled lines in the back of a notebook. I never finished it because I didn't like it. Then in December of 1987 I was due to assist Jim Smith, the evangelist, in a 'Man Alive' meeting at the Colston Hall in Bristol. I'd been asked to contribute two or three pieces which would feed into the general theme of men taking a more dynamic and muscular role in the church. As usual I was panicking because I couldn't quite decide what my third offering should be. Then my wife Bridget discovered my unfinished verses, liked them, and felt sure that they were absolutely right for Jim's meeting. I still had little confidence in the poem, but I had, and always have had, great confidence in my wife's judgement in these matters. I finished the thing off, took it to Bristol with me, and used it at the Colston Hall. Bridget was right.

It's about cost, and if you read it in public, it's worth taking your time. The gaps and pauses are probably more eloquent than the words.

When I Became a Christian

When I became a Christian I said, Lord, now fill me in,
Tell me what I'll suffer in this world of shame and sin.
He said, Your body may be killed, and left to rot and stink,
Do you still want to follow me? I said, Amen!—I think.
I think Amen, Amen I think, I think I say Amen,
I'm not completely sure, can you just run through that
    again?
You say my body may be killed and left to rot and stink,
Well, yes, that sounds terrific, Lord, I say Amen—I think.

But, Lord, there must be other ways to follow you, I said,
I really would prefer to end up dying in my bed.
Well, yes, he said, you could put up with sneers and scorn
    and spit,
Do you still want to follow me? I said, Amen!—a bit.
A bit Amen, Amen a bit, a bit I say Amen,
I'm not entirely sure, can we just run through that again?
You say I could put up with sneers and also scorn and spit,
Well, yes, I've made my mind up, and I say, Amen!—a bit.

Well I sat back and thought a while, then tried a different ploy,
Now, Lord, I said, the Good Book says that Christians live in joy.
That's true, he said, you need the joy to bear the pain and sorrow,
So do you want to follow me? I said, Amen!—tomorrow.
Tomorrow, Lord, I'll say it then, that's when I'll say Amen,
I need to get it clear, can I just run through that again?
You say that I will need the joy, to bear the pain and sorrow,
Well, yes, I think I've got it straight, I'll say, Amen—tomorrow.

He said, Look, I'm not asking you to spend an hour with me,
A quick salvation sandwich and a cup of sanctity,
The cost is you, not half of you, but every single bit,
Now tell me, will you follow me? I said, Amen!—I quit.
I'm very sorry, Lord, I said, I'd like to follow you,
But I don't think religion is a manly thing to do.
He said, Forget religion then, and think about my Son,
And tell me if you're man enough to do what he has done.

Are you man enough to see the need, and man enough to
   go,
Man enough to care for those whom no one wants to know,
Man enough to say the thing that people hate to hear,
To battle through Gethsemane in loneliness and fear.
And listen! Are you man enough to stand it at the end,
The moment of betrayal by the kisses of a friend,
Are you man enough to hold your tongue, and man enough
   to cry,
When nails break your body—are you man enough to die?
Man enough to take the pain, and wear it like a crown,
Man enough to love the world and turn it upside down,
Are you man enough to follow me, I ask you once again.
I said, Oh, Lord, I'm frightened, but I also said Amen.
Amen, Amen, Amen, Amen; Amen, Amen, Amen,
I said, O Lord, I'm frightened, but I also said, Amen.

Books

One christmas I was asked by one of my favourite local churches, Frenchgate Christian Centre in Eastbourne, to put together an 'Entertainment with a message' for the Sunday before Christmas day. It ended up as a collection of sketches and verse linked by a narrator who was searching for Jesus. *Books* is an extract from that presentation, the main body of which can be used separately if the name of the preacher/ pastor/vicar is localised. I've left it in context here to show how it fitted into the general theme, and also to bring eternal fame to Geoff Booker, a good friend of mine who labours unceasingly for Kingsway Publications (he says), and used to attend the church where *Books* was first performed. In fact, as you can tell from the extract, he was supposed to be the one who actually recited the lines, but a rather nasty accident forced him to drop out, so I had to do it. 'Ecclestone' is Ben Ecclestone, an elder at Frenchgate. He has no connection with Kingsway, but plenty of other problems. If you want to use the main section, just substitute your own church leader's name for Ben's.

For the piece to be effective you need *lots* of books, probably forty or fifty, on a table within easy reach of the performer. Careful rehearsal and preparation pay dividends with *Books*.

The point of this piece is not that I believe all Christian paperbacks to be bad or useless. That would be a very strange attitude for a writer of Christian books to adopt. Rather, it is that there are probably too many books, and too much of a tendency on the part of readers to seek final solutions in the printed word. The best Christian books are signposts pointing towards Jesus.

Books

NARRATOR: Excuse me, Mr Booker, sir,
    I'm told—despite your looks—
    You're really rather clever,
    And you're something big in books.
    They say you work for Kingsway.
    Is that right? Do you agree?
GEOFF: Well, yes, except that I would
       say,
    That Kingsway works for me.
NARRATOR: But listen, Mr Booker,
    Could you put us on the track
    Of Jesus? Have you seen him?
    Is he there in paperback?
GEOFF: *(holds up books continually as he speaks)*
    Everything's in paperback!
    All you need to know,
    Little gems of cosmic truth,
    At fifty bob a throw.
    We cover every subject,
    From repentance to the pill,
    If no one's done a book on it,
    We'll find a man who will.
    The formula's a piece of cake,
    It always seems to work:
    'I'm good and happy nowadays,
    I used to be a berk.'
    This one says 'seek unity,
    For heart to heart should speak',
    And this one deals with other faiths,
    And why they're up the creek.
    And if you fear that Ecclestone*
    Is stringing you along,

*Substitute local pastor's name.

Well, this one claims he
　　could be right,
And these five prove he's wrong.
Here's a book that frowns on drink,
But tells you how to search,
For pubs that don't get visited
By people from the church.
Books for Sunday, books for
　　Monday,
Books from north and south,
Books that tell you when to speak
And when to shut your mouth.
Books that don't say very much,
　　(Holds up very thick book)
And books that say a lot,
　　(Holds up very thin book)
Books on why the church is dead,
And books on why it's not.
Books on love and books on praise,
And lots of books on prayer,
Books on how to eat and sleep
And breathe, and wash your hair.
Books on life and death and piles
And drains and constipation,
One on how to tell yourself
You don't like fornication.
Books on washing Christian shirts,
And treating Christian 'flu',
On how to shut the Christian door,
And flush the Christian loo.
Books on sinners, books on saints,
Con-men, cads and crooks,

Books on everything in sight,
There's even books on books.
There's books and books and books
   and books,
And books and books and books,
And books and books and books
   and books
And books and books and books.
Jesus? Well, he's not in stock,
I'll get him – well, I'll try.
But is he fact or fiction?
And who's he published by?
I've got a book *about* him,
Or a pamphlet, or a tract,
He may be here for all I know,
This box is still unpacked.
NARRATOR: No thank you, Mr Booker, sir,
Despite your verbal sprint,
I don't believe I'll find him here,
Perhaps he's out of print.

Nathan Rap

ONE OF THE most dramatic pieces of rubbish-clearing in
the Old Testament section of the Bible must be Nathan the
prophet's confrontation with King David after the Bathsheba
and Uriah incident. David, hitherto a 'man after God's own
heart', summoned the beautiful Bathsheba to his palace one
night, slept with her, and sent her home in the morning.
She became pregnant. Having failed to cover up his
adulterous crime by devious means, he arranged for
Bathsheba's husband, Uriah, an army captain, to be killed on
the field of battle. He then brought the widow back to his
palace and married her himself. How he ever thought he
would escape retribution for these gross infringements of
God's law is difficult to say, except that in my own life, I
know how capable I am of shutting out the voice of
conscience when I want something badly enough.

David did get his come-uppance. Nathan the prophet
told the King a little story about a poor man who lost the
only thing he had. David didn't catch on at all—not until
Nathan explained. Then, he was devastated.

Nathan Rap is the story in verse of that encounter
between Nathan and David. It's actually part of a one-hour
dramatic presentation of the David and Bathsheba story,
involving narration and music, written by myself and James
Hammond who designed this book. This section stands
perfectly well on its own, but it's as well to be familiar with
the story as a whole if you decide to use it. David's story
begins in the sixteenth chapter of the first book of Samuel,
and finishes with his death in the second chapter of the first
book of Kings. An amazingly detailed account of an
extraordinary life.

Nathan Rap

It was evening in the palace when the prophet came by,
There was trouble in his manner, there was thunder in his
    eye,
He was still for a moment, he was framed in the door,
And the king said, 'Nathan! . . . What are you here for?'
The prophet said, 'David, I've a tale to tell,'
So the king sat and listened as the darkness fell,
While the hard-eyed prophet took a seat and began,
The story of a merciless and evil man.

'This man,' said Nathan, 'had a mountain of gold,
Sheep by the thousand he bought and sold,
He never said, "Can I afford it or not?"
What this man wanted, this man got!
And one thing he wanted, and he wanted real bad,
Was the only living thing that a poor man had,
And he knew that it was wrong, but he took it just the same.'
'I'll kill him!' said the king, 'Just tell me his name!'

'It was a lamb,' said the prophet, 'just a little baby lamb,
But he saw it and he took it and he didn't give a damn,
And he knew that it was special, and he knew it was a friend,
And he knew about the sadness that would never, never
    end,
And that same man began to plan a far more evil thing.'
Then David rose and cried aloud, 'He'll reckon with the
    king!'
'So do you think,' said Nathan, 'we should stop his little
    game?'
'I'll smash him!' shouted David, 'tell me his name!'

'Be careful,' said the prophet, 'don't go overboard,'
For David's eyes were shining like the blade of a sword,
'Perhaps you should be merciful, perhaps you should try
To understand the man before you say he must die.'
But David said, 'I understand that wrong is always wrong,
I am the king, I must defend the weak against the strong.'
Then Nathan questioned softly, 'So this man must take the
    blame?'
And the king was screaming, 'Nathan! Will you tell me his
    name?'

Then a silence fell upon them like the silence of a tomb,
The prophet nodded slowly as he moved across the room,
And, strangely, as he came he grew more awesome and
    more wise,
And when he looked at David there was sadness in his eyes.
But David's anger burned in him, he drew his sword and
    said,
'I swear, before the dawn has come, that sinner will be
    dead!
No more delay, no mercy talk, give me his name!' he cried,
Then Nathan said, 'It's you, it's you!' and the king just died.

Away in a Gutter

A Father Knows No Sadness

I'VE HAD THE same problems with my reaction to starvation in the Third World as most people, I imagine. I find it very difficult to unjumble all the thoughts and feelings that are provoked by pictures of dying children and despairing communities. 'So what?' say some, 'your terrible unjumbling problems are of very little interest to kids who'll be dead next week unless someone does something. Get your wallet out!'

Of course that's true; how can it not be? And yet I can't help feeling that, when it comes to Christians, unless their desire to give arises from a real understanding of and identification with the suffering Christ, then psychological and spiritual gears have a tendency to crunch horribly. The twenty-fifth chapter of Matthew's gospel explains it, and Mother Theresa's words, 'He has no hands but our hands . . .' express it perfectly. So does her life.

Away in a Gutter and *A Father Knows No Sadness* are trying to highlight the two essential facts that Jesus is in the dying child, and that if we truly love one, we will soon learn to love the other.

Away in a Gutter should be sung just as 'Away in a Manger' is sung, preferably by a single child or small group of children. *A Father Knows No Sadness* fits well to the tune of 'Oh, Jesus I have promised', and can simply be sung as a hymn.

Away in a Gutter

Away in a gutter
No food and no bed
The little Lord Jesus
Hangs down his sweet head
The stars in the bright sky
Look down and they say
The little Lord Jesus
Is wasting away.

We love you Lord Jesus
We hope you survive
We'll see you tomorrow
If you're still alive
You won't live for long now
With no tender care
You're best off in heaven
We'll see you up there.

The darkness is lifting
The baby awakes
But little Lord Jesus
No movement he makes
No flesh on his body
No light in his eye
The little Lord Jesus
Is going to die.

A Father Knows No Sadness

A father knows no sadness,
No deeper-searching pain,
Than children who have taken,
But will not give again.
What profit from his loving,
If love is never shared,
What insult to his giving,
If nothing can be spared?

They wait for our remembrance,
The ones who live in need,
The ones our father trusts us
To shelter and to feed.
And if you truly love him,
Then they are precious too,
And if they are a burden,
That burden is for you.

And one day when he asks us,
To say what we have done,
Our answers will go flying
Towards the setting sun.
And how we shall remember
The truth that we were told,
As every word that leaves us
Is burned, or turned to gold.

Snowdon

As a NEWLY converted teenager I experienced quite deep feelings of hostility towards the man who wrote the book of James in the New Testament. Fancy spoiling all that comfortable 'justified by faith' stuff by talking about works! Why on earth did the man have to go defining religion as 'staying untainted by the world and helping widows and orphans?' I fancied I could see James in my mind's eye. A sort of no-nonsense sports-master type who thought poetry was cissy and words were things to be hurled around like sports equipment. I wanted to stay enjoyably embroiled in the theory, not complicate things by getting involved in the practice.

It's so easy to get locked into an endless round of (quite laudable) religious exercises, and never actually do anything. Nowadays James is one of my favourite books, and I think the writer has a lot more poetry in him than I ever realised.

Snowdon is an adaptation of 'Letter to William', a story from my book *The Final Boundary*. I suppose it's really about facing the true cost of following Jesus. Quite a challenge.

The directions that I've included are only suggestions of course, but it is important that the lights fade to nothing at the end of Angerage's final speech and that the two characters are frozen until all is blacked out.

Snowdon

*A man is working at a desk. There is nothing special about him.
He looks pleasant enough. An empty chair awaits visitors on the
other side of the desk. There is a knock on the door. The man,
whose name is Bill Angerage, looks up.*

ANGERAGE: (*brightly*) Come in, just push!

VAUGHN: (*enters nervously, holding a piece of paper*) Mister
er . . . Angerage?

ANGERAGE: (*gets up and comes across to greet him*) Bill
Angerage. Call me Bill. You must be Mister Vaughn. Right?

VAUGHN: Yes, that's right, I er . . . phoned earlier to make an
er . . . appointment.

ANGERAGE: (*gestures towards the spare chair and resumes his
own seat*) Take a seat and relax, Mister Vaughn. What's
your first name?

VAUGHN: Er . . . Timothy—Tim.

ANGERAGE: Okay, Tim. Fire away! What can we help you with?

VAUGHN: (*unfolds his piece of paper as he speaks*) Well, you
see—I just happened to see your er . . . your
er . . .

ANGERAGE: (*smiles and nods*) Our announcement?

VAUGHN: Yes, your announcement. I just happened to see
your announcement in the paper, and—well at first I
thought it was a joke—

ANGERAGE: No joke, Tim.

VAUGHN: Yes-no-well, that's what I wasn't sure about. I kept
reading it over and over again, and the more I read it, the
more I thought I'd better make sure. It seemed a bit . . .
(*he reads from the piece of paper carefully*) 'United Kingdom
Christian recruitment Centre. We are now the *sole*
(*emphasises 'sole'*) agents for salvation et al in England,
Wales, Scotland and Northern Ireland. Visitors warmly

welcomed. Please ring Freephone ZAP for quick
appointments. Caution: previous arrangements may *not*
be valid. We will advise with pleasure.' (*Looks up
worriedly.*)

ANGERAGE: And that we will, Tim. And more than happy to do
so. (*Beams.*)

VAUGHN: Thank you. The thing is Mister Ang—

ANGERAGE: Bill!

VAUGHN: The thing is, er . . . Bill, that I really *do* want to be a
Christian—

ANGERAGE: (*interrupts, leaping to his feet*) Tim, that's great!
(*Comes round the desk and almost hugs Tim in his delight.
His pleasure is totally genuine.*) That is really wonderful
news! I can't tell you how it makes me feel to hear those
words. Thank you so much for letting me be the one to
hear them. Let me shake your hand! (*He pumps his hand.*)

VAUGHN: (*somewhat overwhelmed*) Thanks Mist—Bill, I'm glad
you're pleased—actually, I er . . . sort of thought I already
was one. I go to a church that's quite lively, and I've made
a commitment and I go to a Bible-study group, and I
pray—a bit, and we have the gifts and outreach and—and
er . . . all that, so (*looks at paper again*) I don't quite see . . .

ANGERAGE: (*nodding seriously. Moves back to his chair*) Tim,
let's get down to business. As you've probably gathered
from reading this little announcement of ours in the
paper, things have changed a lot—radically I might say.
The whole caboodle of prayer, Bible-study, church
services et cetera has been scrapped. (*Tim is about to
interrupt.*) Direct orders from HQ, Tim.

VAUGHN: You mean . . .? (*Points ceiling-wards.*)

ANGERAGE: (*nods solemnly*) Direct orders, Tim. All that stuff
goes out the window. No need any more for discussions

about salvation by faith, or about who's in or who's out.
The whole thing's been completely redesigned. You can
still get (*counts them off on one hand*) total forgiveness,
eternal life, love, joy, and peace, the whole package as
before, but the terms are different—very different.

VAUGHN: But, Mister Angerage—

ANGERAGE: Call me Bill, Tim, there's a good chap.

VAUGHN: Bill, all those things you said don't matter any
more—if we don't have those—I mean, what's left? What
do we have to do?

ANGERAGE: Aah, well! Now we come to it, Tim my friend.
What indeed? Listen—all you have to do now is climb
Snowdon three times every week! (*Leans back.*)
   (*Long pause*)

VAUGHN: (*stunned*) Snowdon . . .

ANGERAGE: Yep!

VAUGHN: Three times . . .

ANGERAGE: Every week! That's the long and short and the top
and the bottom of it, Tim my friend.

VAUGHN: But . . . why?

ANGERAGE: Ours not to reason why, mate. If HQ says that's
the way it's to be done, then that's the way it's to be done.
Faith! That's what you need. The instructions are very
simple. Snowdon—three times a week.

VAUGHN: And there's no other way to get forgiveness and
peace and—all the rest?

ANGERAGE: (*slowly*) No other way, my friend. Worth it
though—isn't it?

VAUGHN: Oh, yes—yes, of course. (*Pauses, then bursts out*) But
what happens about my job, Bill? I work a hundred miles
away from Snowdon. I mean, I wouldn't be able to carry
on with what I'm doing now, would I? Good heavens . . .

it must take a day to climb right up Snowdon and down again, so that means three days *plus* the travelling. I'd hardly have time to do anything, let alone get a decent job of any sort. I wouldn't have any money. I wouldn't—

ANGERAGE: Any savings, Tim?

VAUGHN: I've got a few thousand in the building society, yes, but I didn't want to touch that until . . . (*A fresh thought*) What about friends? How do I keep up with my friends? I'll hardly ever see them—they'll think I've gone mad. They'll think . . . Look Bill—Mister Angerage (*Angerage raises a finger*)—Bill, this doesn't seem right. All you have to do in the church I'm in is make a personal commitment and get baptised by immersion. You don't have to go anywhere or do anything much . . .

ANGERAGE: (*kindly*) Tim, don't you think the travelling, or even living down in Wales itself might be worth it if you get eternal life and happiness in return? After all, you've come to see me today, so it must mean something to you. You've got this far, mate.

VAUGHN: (*ponders*) Do some people come to see you and then decide not to . . . go ahead then?

ANGERAGE: (*sighs deeply*) The vast majority, I'm sad to say. Some of 'em try to compromise, despite the fact that I always make it quite clear that the three climbs are an absolute base-line minimum.

VAUGHN: (*interested despite himself*) How do they compromise then?

ANGERAGE: Well, there's one church north of here for instance. The minister came down to see me—he'd seen that announcement just like you—said he agreed with everything I told him, went off happily back home and wrote me a letter a few weeks later to say he'd discussed the whole thing with the church council and they'd come up with an *inspired* idea. They hired a carpenter to construct a four-foot high model of Snowdon with two steps going up one side, and two going down the other. They've built it into the service. It comes just between the third hymn and the sermon.

VAUGHN: (*hopefully*) And that doesn't count?

ANGERAGE: It's not climbing Snowdon three times a week.

(*There is a pause. Vaughn is about to say something but changes his mind. He takes a biro and a piece of paper from his pocket and starts jotting something. Angerage waits patiently. At last Vaughn looks up with hopeful enthusiasm.*)

VAUGHN: Bill, listen! I've just been thinking. There must be other jobs that need doing besides the actual climbing. Supposing I adapted all the choruses we sing at the moment so that they fit the new way of things? (*He is suddenly inspired.*) We could call it the Snowdon Songbook!

(*Bill slowly shakes his head, but Vaughn is quite carried away now.*)

Look, I've just been trying one or two out. Er . . . this one for instance. Hallelujah I'm a Christian—you know the one I mean. This is what it sounds like when it's changed. Listen—listen! (*He sings, referring to his notes sometimes.*)

Hallelujah, I'm a climber,
I climb all day,
I climb up Snowdon,
Climb all the way,
Hallelujah, I'm a climber,
I climb all day.

ANGERAGE: (*gently*) Tim, I don't think—

VAUGHN: Just a minute! Just a minute! What d'you think about this one? Used to be Marching to Zion. Listen! (*Sings again—rather feverishly*)

We're marching to Snowdon,
Beautiful, beautiful Snowdon,
We're marching upward to Snowdon,
The beautiful mountain of God.

And what about this one . . .?

What a friend we have in Snowdon,
All our climbing gear we wear,
What a—

ANGERAGE: (*interrupts with great authority*) No, Tim! It's no good simply singing about it. You've got to *do* it! You've *got* to climb Snowdon three times every week! (*Stands and takes a pace or two before speaking again.*) Why, I could take you to a town only a few miles from here where they've set up Snowdon counselling services, Snowdon discussion groups, and courses in the real meaning of climbing. But none of them actually do it! One of our chaps who comes from that same town, and pops up from Wales very occasionally, isn't allowed into any of those groups because he's 'in error' with his simplistic approach to Snowdon. No, Tim, if you want to write some songs to keep you going while you're on the slopes, then that's fine—good idea in fact. But not instead of! Won't wash with HQ you see.

VAUGHN: (*pathetically*) I don't even like travelling much.

ANGERAGE: Well, its up—

VAUGHN: (*slapping the table in triumph*) I'm not fit! I won't get up there—not even once! It's not fair! What about that?

ANGERAGE: (*he's heard it all before*) All you've got to do is turn up and climb as far as you can; and we'll make sure you get to the top from there, even if you have to be carried to the nearest mountain railway stop. Don't worry! Young chap like you, you'll be fit as a fiddle in no time. Wouldn't surprise me if you were nearly running up inside a fortnight.

VAUGHN: Do I have to decide now, Bill? I'm not quite . . .

ANGERAGE: Look, Tim, you go off home, have a good think about it and let me know what you decide. If you want to go ahead we'll give you a hand with the practical side. Okay?

VAUGHN: (*gets up. Moves slowly towards the door. Angerage follows him.*) All right, Bill, I'll go home and—and think about it.

ANGERAGE: (*shakes Vaughn's hand and opens the door*) Good to meet you, Tim, I'm sure you'll make the right decision.

VAUGHN: (*bursting out just as he is about to exit.*) I just don't see what was so wrong with the old way anyway! The people in my church never did anyone any harm! Why do you want to go and make it all much harder?

ANGERAGE: You really haven't understood at all, have you Tim? We haven't made it harder—we've made it much much easier . . .

Fade down to darkness

Daffodils
Gatwick Airport
Winter Walk
I Watch

THE FOLLOWING FOUR short poems are all, in their own way, expressions of hope or optimism. *Daffodils* is simply a tribute to one of the most beautiful things I know. I'm crazy about flowers. My wife quite often buys me a bunch of cut blooms to put on my desk while I write. What's that got to do with God? 'Whatsoever is lovely . . .' Every now and then you encounter Christians who are wary about 'undue appreciation' of natural things. For me, a walk over the Downs in the middle of an autumn sunset says more about a personal loving God than most sermons.

Gatwick Airport is the result of simply sitting in the middle of passenger bustle, enjoying the complexity and variety of what's going on around me. I love Gatwick. A restless village. In the middle of it all there's a chapel for anybody to use. I'm sure it *is* used, but I've never seen anyone else in there. It seems so right, though, that there is a still heart in the centre of such a busy place.

Winter Walk: I've so enjoyed watching my children as they discover wonderful things for the first time. One of the things I often ask God to renew in me is that capacity for wonder and enjoyment of simple pleasures, especially the free ones. Perhaps I'll be fitted with fresh, non-rust enjoyment apparatus when I get to heaven. I hope so.

I Watch reflects an important dawn in my life, at a time when I had thought the night was going to be very long indeed. It came as rather a shock to realise that God must be at *least* as nice as my mother . . .

Daffodils

Daffodils are not flowers.
They are natural neon from the dark earth,
Precious metal grown impatient,
Beaten, shaped, and dipped in pools
Of ancient, sunken light.
Folded, packed, and parachuted through,
To stand and dumbly trumpet out
The twice triumphant sun.

Gatwick Airport

Sad, robotic, angel voices
Softly, sweetly speaking
To a thousand restless souls
Of gateways and departures
To a hundred different lands,
That may flow with milk and honey
Or lay heavy on the spirit
Like the old Egyptian sands.

Winter Walk

I wish I was my son again,
The first in all the world to know
The cornflake crunch of frosted grass
Beside the polar paving stones,
Beneath the drip of liquid light
From watercolour winter suns.

I Watch

I watch
Frightened
Helpless
But secretly willing
As my foot rises, moving forward with my weight,
And I realise
That at last
I am going to walk.

Shades of Blue

I WAS ONCE introduced at a meeting as 'Adrian Plass, who some of us may feel asks more questions than he provides answers for.' A doubtful recommendation on the face of it, but thinking the comment over afterwards I felt more relieved than otherwise. Anyone who's been involved in public Christian work knows how easy it is to paper over the cracks in one's own understanding of faith and present a shiny and possibly intimidating 'wonderfulness' to folk who are often all too ready to sink into a slough of spiritual inferiority. You have to be careful, though, if you do try to avoid the shiny path of cubed spirituality. The truth is not very popular in some parts of the church. But then that's always been the case, hasn't it?

The other thing that comforted me about that introductory comment was the reflection that Jesus prefaced many of his remarks with a question rather than a statement. 'What think ye . . .?'

Shades of Blue is a whimsical attempt to show how God is quietly present even in the half-light of my temperament. Four out of the five verses are questions, and the fifth is not exactly 'call to the front' material, but it is true, and it reflects the awareness I have nowadays that he is always there, gently caring.

Shades of Blue

Does winter end in seaside towns
When councils paint anew
The railings on the promenade
In hopeful shades of blue?

And if the tide loved Brighton beach
Would God come down and say
With gentle hands upon the surf
'You need not turn today'?

Will massive Church of England bells
Have faith enough to ring
And overcome their weariness
When they believe in Spring?

Are there machines for measuring
The power of my prayers
And anyway, and anyway,
And anyway, who cares?

I think you care, but gently,
I think, because you do,
The colour of my sadness
Is a hopeful shade of blue.

I Want to Be with You

THE PHRASE 'praise and worship' has jelled in my consciousness like 'Morecambe and Wise', or 'Fish and Chips'. After you've used and heard the same phrase thousands of times it becomes oddly meaningless. I don't mean that I don't like doing it. I do. I especially like silent or musically accompanied meditative praise and worship. I like singing choruses, as long as I don't get told off about what I'm doing with my face or my feet. I like singing hymns and meaning them. I sometimes like speaking 'praise and worship' to God, if the words come naturally. That's the problem for me, and it applies to most religious/spiritual activities. How do you stay natural? What is a genuine statement to God going to sound like? How do I stop things like 'praise-and-worship' coagulating into meaningless lumps of activity?

This issue crystallised for me in 1986, when, as a member of CAFE, the Christian Arts Fellowship in Eastbourne, I was involved in the writing of a Christian revue for production in one of the local theatres. We needed a final song—something that completely avoided religious clichés, but was nevertheless a strong and honest statement of faith and hope. I dug into myself as far as I dared, and produced *I Want to Be with You*, a mixture of doubt, entreaty, fear and hope. It really was what I felt I would want to say to God when the crunch came. The bottom line was 'HELP!'.

The verses were spoken over a pre-recorded musical backing, the chorus ('I want to be with you' repeated eight times) was sung. One day I'd love to do this song with a large choir or congregation joining in with the chorus.

There's no harm in finding out what your spiritual bottom line is and putting it into words. Try it!

I Want to Be with You

WORDS & MUSIC: ADRIAN PLASS

When the streamer has sailed
And my journey has failed
When the switches are on
But the power has gone
When I open my eyes
But the sun doesn't rise
When it's dark on the screen
Where the picture has been
When there's nobody there
To pretend that they care
When it comes to the end
And I long for a friend
When I wish that I knew
What the hell I should do
I want to be with you

I want to be with you. (× 8)

When the people I've known
Have gone and left me alone
When the things that I said
Are sounding empty and dead
When I reach for the phone
But it's dead as a stone
When my talk about God
Is feeling foolish and odd
When the thoughts in my mind
Have left my feelings behind
When the skin on my hand
Becomes as dry as the sand
When the pain in my heart
Begins to tear me apart
Will I remember what's true?
I hope I know what to do
I want to be with you.

I want to be with you. (× 8)

When the silence has come
And the singers are dumb
When we stand in the light
And it's pointless to fight
When I see what they find
In the back of my mind
When there's no one to blame
For the sin and the shame
When I wait for the word
To let me fly like a bird
But I fear in my heart
I wouldn't know how to start
When the tears in my eyes
Are blurring over the skies
When I suddenly claim
To remember your name
When I see that it's you
Coming out of the blue
I want to be with you.

I want to be with you. (× 8)

Letter to Lucifer

Letter to Lucifer is a literary device, not a spiritual one. It's important to make that point because, although I think that letters to God are an excellent idea, I'm very much less sure about the advisability of writing to the devil. I don't want a reply. This then is *what* I would write, *if* I wrote, not an actual attempt to communicate with the devil.

I conclude this book with it because it sums up so much that I've wanted and tried to say. Things about deception and confusion and, especially, things about Jesus, who became a piece of human rubbish so that we could become clean. May we all understand and appreciate that a little more each day.

Letter to Lucifer

Dear Lucifer,

I've been out walking in the rain today. One of those mellow spring showers, falling in big, splashy, warm drops—like the tears that Alice shed when she grew too tall for Wonderland—and I thought of you.

Now, I'm well aware that when this letter was put into your hands, the first thing you did was to flick through the pages until you came to my signature at the end. Then, I should imagine, you slapped the paper, threw your head back and laughed like a drain. What a scream! That clown Plass attempting some feeble communication with His Infernal Majesty. Plass, who—over the last twenty years or so—has provided such a rich and consistent source of entertainment for you and yours.

Plass, who has become almost institutionalised into a devils' training ground, where even the most unskilled, love-besmirched little novice could hardly do him less good than he does himself. No doubt you've called a few of the lads over to listen as you read out what is bound to be real laugh-a-minute stuff. Well, gather round by all means, chaps. You will have a few laughs, but—there's something else as well.

First of all, and I'm sure you remember it well, there was my 'conversion' back in the sixties. You lot found the word 'conversion' a real rib-tickler back in those days, didn't you? Cheap salvation, cut-price Christianity, lots of happy-ever-after talk, and a minefield of guilt and failure to stumble through afterwards. Oh, it was real enough to start with. God called me that day as surely as if he'd blown a trumpet, clear and sweet, from the sky. (Did you read *that* bit out loud, Lucifer?) But after that you took over and—yes, you really screwed me up. You made sure that no one talked to me about cost and depth and maturity, and, above all, you used every device you knew to hide from me the fact (and it is a fact, Lucifer) that God is very *nice*, and he *likes* me. You never minded me using words like 'marvellous' and 'omnipotent', or phrases like 'everlasting love', and 'Holy Redeemer'. They just increased my inadequacy—made me feel even more small and wretched. You did a good job, let's face it. In the end I saw God as a cross between a headmaster and a bank manager, and my miserable self as a wicked little schoolboy with a horrendous overdraft.

Yes, all right, have a good laugh. Cackle away, fellers! I can see it from your point of view. Good piece of work; a really solid platform for the building of a lifetime of confusion and pretence. Because I went on to do what so many others do, didn't I? I tried to copy the people and the behaviour that I saw around me. Hands in the air, leaping about, impassioned singing, shouts of 'Hallelujah!' and 'Praise the Lord!' I was like a big half-witted puppet, and there's not much doubt about who was pulling the strings either, is there, Lucifer? You really worked me! Up and down and round and round and to and fro I went.

But I'm sure the time you liked best, the bit of my day that you really licked your lips over, was that moment when I finally got home at night, and I was on my own. Suddenly, as I walked through my own front door—your timing was always perfect—you would just let go of the strings, and everything in me would crumple and collapse. All my words, my spiritual effusions, my confident references to 'the Lord', became nothing but lines in a performance, embarrassing in their hollowness. I'll bet I was your own special little nightly soap opera—something to put your feet up and enjoy without effort.

Did you get a little round of applause when you read out that last bit, Lucifer? You deserve it. You did well.

Of course, *I* couldn't understand it at all. Why didn't God come home with me at night? Why did I only believe in him when I was surrounded by other Christians? Why, Lucifer, I hardly believed in my *own* existence, let alone God's! I felt like a hologram, a projection of the feelings and attitudes and reactions of others. No real substance of my own, nothing to hang on to and feel safe. It was a nightmare for me and a triumph for you. Once again you had succeeded in performing one of the neatest tricks of all; taking a person who had 'become a Christian' and making him more abjectly miserable than before. And the supreme joke of it all—from your point of view that is—was that if I blamed anyone, it wasn't you, it was God. Everything was God's fault! He was a nasty, harsh, narrow moralist who had little time to waste on weaklings and sinners like me.

It took me twenty years to see through the lies you told me then. Twenty years of spiritual switch-back riding. Up to the peaks, and down—way down—to the troughs. Brittle ecstasy or clogging despair, but mostly despair. And yet— something else was happening as well.

Far be it from me to offer you advice, Lucifer, but if I were you I'd dismiss that little audience of yours at this point. The next bit won't be too good for morale.

You see, the something else was Jesus. Go on, read that name out good and loud. Jesus! Shout it so loud that it trumpets through hell like an obscenity in a convent. I'm talking, of course, about the *real* Jesus, not the Weary Willie, nor the vindictive hardcase, that your publicity department has had so much success with.

He stayed with me through all those years. Granted, he

was often little more than the faintest of nightlights in the darkness, but the point is, Lucifer, he was there; greater than the foolishness of church institutions; greater than my sins and silliness; greater than any attempt to leave him behind, and in the end, Lucifer, greater—much greater—than you. I've been reading about him in the gospels and seeing him properly for the first time.

For years I was one of the millions who think they've read and understood about that incredible three-year ministry, but I hadn't, not really—you saw to that. In fact, you've managed to divert huge numbers of present-day Christians away from the first four books of the New Testament, haven't you? You've got them combing minutely through all sorts of other books, squeezing individual verses, or even words, to extract tiny, gelatinous drops of meaning. All very important and useful no doubt, but useful to *you* as well, as long as it distracts them from seeing the broad and beautiful picture of God walking the earth as a real man.

So *real*, Lucifer! Such a lover of natural things, such a mixture of all the emotions, such a despiser of sin, such a tender and compassionate lover of the small people and sinners who had nothing to offer him but their own need. Such a brave sufferer at the end when friendship and the richness of life said 'Stay', but destiny and obedience said that the cross could not be avoided. He was and is a good chap, Lucifer, and I love him. Oh, I know I'll go on making mistakes! And I know you won't give up. I know that every time I find a genuine pearl of truth you're going to send a bin-load of rubbish tumbling down to bury and obscure it. That's a real winner with people like me who so easily step backwards into cynicism. But I *am* learning—learning to ignore me and listen to him. A small, quiet sureness has taken root in me, and I'm relying on him to make sure that it grows.

The thing is, Lucifer, that I've been down in the dark for a long time. I've tasted hell, and I know what it is. It's the fear, the knowledge in your case, that God will never be able to smile at you again, that you've lost the only thing really worth having—the love of God. And I know now why you are so bitterly, cruelly determined to prevent as many as possible from finding peace. It's because you've lost it, isn't it? You wanted more than it's possible to have, and you lost everything. Jesus will never smile at you again, and all that's left is the endless striving to suck others into the loveless vacuum that you inhabit.

But out in the rain, just now, I was thinking. In the night (are there darker, deeper nights in endless night?) do you ever discover in yourself enough microscopic traces of shame and longing to make up a single tear of genuine remorse, no bigger, perhaps, than one of those fertile drops of rain falling so copiously on and around me? If so, then I think that even you could be saved, Lucifer. I fear, though, that the last spot of moisture dried and disappeared in you a very long time ago.

I remain, through God's grace, Never Yours,
    Adrian Plass